Live the Dream

Become rich and free through your business

Joan Baker

ALLEN&UNWIN

First published in 2006

Allen & Unwin
83 Alexander Street
Crows Nest NSW 2065
Australia
Phone: (61 2) 8425 0100
Fax: (61 2) 9906 2218
Email: info@allenandunwin.com
Web: www.allenandunwin.com

National Library of Australia
Cataloguing-in-Publication entry:

Baker, Joan, 1956- .
    Live the dream : become rich and free through your business.
    ISBN 978 1 74114 807 7.

ISBN 1 74114 807 3.

1. Success in business. 2. Quality of work life. I. Title.

650.1

Typeset in 12/14 pt Adobe Garamond by Midland Typesetters, Australia
Printed in Australia by McPherson's Printing Group

10 9 8 7 6 5 4 3 2 1

Contents

Joan welcomes inquiries and feedback from readers and can be contacted at <jbaker@wealthcoaches.net>.

Introduction

Business doesn't matter: it's the quality of your life that matters. Business is only a tool to create the wealth that gives us wonderful lives.

Wealth is essential for good lives. The most common and most successful route to wealth has always been business ownership. A business has the capacity to create the wealth to set you free to live the life of your dreams.

You already have a dream. You know what kind of life you want for yourself and your loved ones. That dream is what you are striving for and why you picked up this book.

Your business is only a vehicle to deliver your dream. But you have to get the vehicle right—the business has to perform. When businesses perform, they deliver wonderful returns for owners; when they don't perform, the end result is failure and the journey can be very painful for all concerned. Many businesses just struggle along, earning little money and requiring huge effort. Your life is too important to run a business like that.

This book is about getting your business right so that it will perform well enough to give you the life you want. You have to get the basic model right so your business is capable of creating wealth. Then you need to focus on making it as profitable as you can. Ultimately, the business needs to deliver enough wealth, either through sustainable profits or the sale of the business, to set you free to live your perfect life.

1

Creating wealth and freedom

The way it is

I meet a lot of people who own and run a business. They are a diverse group. Some have left their jobs in search of the independence of self-employment and are largely doing the same job as before except that they are now the boss—and in charge of everything! Others have set up businesses with partners or employees and are now very busy juggling the many roles and responsibilities that make up the life of the entrepreneur. All of them began with great optimism, convinced that they would make it big—after all, the whole point of setting up a business is to become rich and free. It's risky leaving a good steady job with a regular pay packet, so why do people do it? In different ways, people tell me the same story over and over again: *they want wealth and freedom.*

Most of the self-employed and business owners I meet can speak passionately of the life that they longed for when they gave up their jobs and went out on their own. They can wax lyrical about the success they dreamed of, the achievements they would have and, above all, the eventual lifestyle. Most foresaw having enough money and time to enjoy full lives, freed from the shackles of work.

However, the reality for many of them is far from the dream. I get to meet these people in seminars or as a business coach because they are not making enough money or they now have no life at all due to the long hours they work. Many have both problems! Some are not selling enough or not making enough profit. Others have cash-flow problems. Sometimes marriages are in trouble and the kids hardly see their mother or father. The business owner is wedded to the business, worrying and working night and day, with no time for anything else. They have become obsessed with their various business problems and have lost sight of why they started in business in the first place.

How are *you* doing? Are you making plenty of money? Do you have enough time to live the life that you want? Are you creating a valuable business that someday you can sell? Will you ever have enough money and enough time to stop and live the life you want? After all, this is why you are in business—to create the wealth that will give you the security and freedom to spend your time as you choose. You wanted freedom—and you know you won't have any financial freedom until you have enough wealth and enough time to take back your life. Business is simply a means to an end and business owners should make sure that their business performs well enough to give them wealth and freedom.

Financial freedom

Financial freedom is that happy state where both your money and your time are your own—you have enough money to live the life you want and you no longer need to work to earn it. Your money is your own in the sense that you have low or no borrowings. Your time is your own in that you no longer need to drive your business hard on a daily basis.

The whole point of setting up and running a business is to end up financially free. The business exists to create enough wealth to eventually set you free—hopefully sooner rather than later. There are plenty of people who are wealthy but not financially free. These people often have very valuable businesses, and therefore high net worth, but they are still carrying large debts and are still working many hours a week. Financial freedom means having enough wealth invested to give you sufficient income to live the life you want without risk and with little work. Your business should make you wealthy, but you need to be thinking right from the start about the endgame—and for most people the endgame is financial freedom.

Let's take stock. You wouldn't be reading this if you were blissfully happy with your business and your life, so let's start with an audit of where you are.

How is your business doing? The numbers don't lie, so you should focus on those. Write everything down—it will make it more real and you will need these numbers as a base for your new plans.

- What profits did you make last year? Profits $_____
- How much did you pay yourself? Salary/wage $_____
- How much were you able to take out of the business after your salary? Drawings or dividends $_____
- How much was reinvested in the business? Reinvested $_____
- What do you think the business would be worth if you sold it today? Estimated business value $_____

And what about the rest of your finances:

- What else do you own—house, holiday home, shares, investment property? House value + Holiday home value + Other assets + Business value = Assets $_____

- What do you owe—business loans, mortgage, credit card debt? Mortgage + Business loans + Other debts = Liabilities $_____
- **Assets – Liabilities = Net worth $_____**

Your net worth number is the amount of wealth you have accumulated at this point.

To be financially free, you need to accumulate enough wealth to live the life you want without having to go to work every day to create income.

Time and money

Many business owners have one but not the other. The diagram below shows that those who are financially free have lots of money *and* lots of time. Their time is their own because they no longer have to work for income. Their investments give them enough passive income to allow them the lifestyle they choose. Business owners set out to be wealthy and free—after all, that is what a business is for. Unfortunately, many owners end up without enough money or without enough time—or without either, trapped in a business that consumes all of their time and does not make them enough money.

Low income/lot of time

While many business owners have low income, few have plenty of time. Some who find they have lots of time on their hands (for example, the self-employed who are contracting or consulting) may have far too much 'free' time because they are not getting enough work. This is not leisure time, of course, as they spend it worrying about the work that they should be attracting. In addition, these business owners may be making far too little money to use the time well. They are less time-pressured for all the wrong reasons—the phone isn't ringing, their products and services are not in demand, their business isn't growing. They do not have enough money, either—and their beloved venture is probably dying before their eyes. Right now, these people may be considering shelving their dreams, swallowing their pride and looking for a 'proper job' in order to pay the mounting bills.

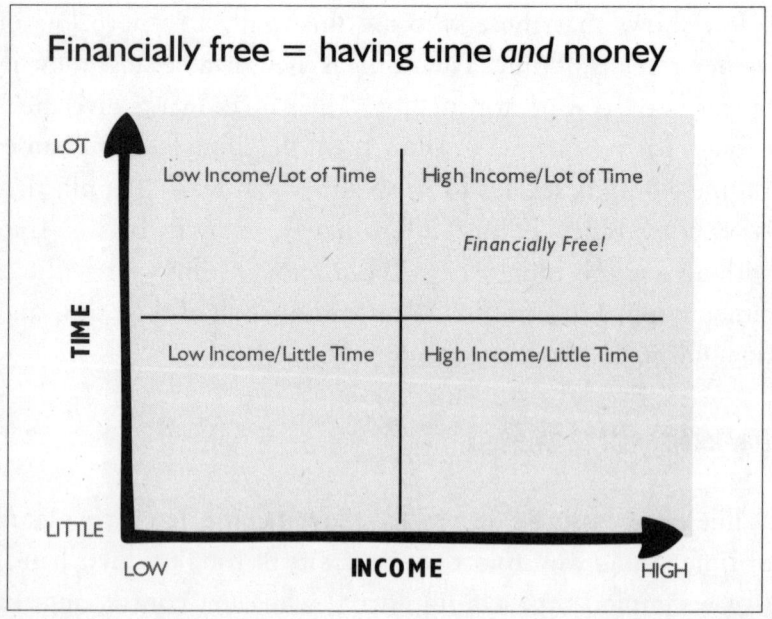

Jim left his well-paid corporate job as a Development Manager over two years ago. He has a passion for training and wanted to do his own thing. At the same time, he moved his wife Marie and their two children to another city for family reasons—Marie's parents were not managing very well, owing to ill health. Jim is struggling to get enough work and earn sufficient income to support the family. He has plenty of time on his hands, but it is the wrong sort of time— he cannot relax and use it for leisure as he is so worried about getting work. In spite of his best endeavours, his income is way below what he earned in his previous job.

Low income/little time

Some people have neither time nor money because nothing is working in their business. In fact, they are frantic with worry and wondering if they are about to lose everything—their business, the family home, their health and marriage. These people are usually running around in circles trying to plug holes, trying to get money in, trying to prevail on their suppliers and the bank for further credit. This is a terrible way to live.

Frank owns his own garage. He has always been absorbed by motors and machines of all kinds and couldn't wait to leave school and work through his apprenticeship. After several years as a top mechanic for someone else, Frank set up on his own. He has good premises and has another mechanic and two apprentices working for him now. Frank's problem is that he is very busy six—and sometimes seven— days a week. He can hardly remember when he last had a holiday, as no one in his team is competent to mind the shop while he's away. His family used to complain endlessly about him never being at home; now they have given up complaining, which is almost worse. He struggles to attract staff, as there is a long-term shortage of skilled tradespeople. Apprentices tend to move on once they are trained. They are attracted to overseas travel or bigger cities with larger workshops. Frank is exhausted and almost depressed. No matter how hard he works, he doesn't seem to make any headway. To add to his problems, his profits are low. He wonders what he is doing wrong—after all, he would earn almost as much working for someone else, without any of the hassle or worries and with far fewer hours.

High income/little time

Some business owners are bringing in quite good money. The business is thriving and profits are good. The business is over the early, scary, survival times and the owners have uncovered good opportunities for growth. However, their lives are consumed by the business. They work long hours and their partners have to look after their home life and social life alone. They frequently break promises to family and friends, missing school visits, camps, celebrations. Holidays? What holidays? The way the business is set up does not allow—or so they believe—for them to be away. Finding yourself in this position is a big trap. On the surface, it looks like you have made it. You may even be able to afford quite a high standard of living for your family—a better home, good cars, private schools, all the trappings. However, there is a huge price to pay in health, relationships and quality of life.

> Jane has her own real estate business. She has worked hard over the years to understand her market and become well known in her locality. Profits have been good for several years—the boom in the market has coincided with the establishment of her business. Jane has several agents to organise, train and keep productive. It's a seven-day-a-week business—and you can't turn clients away when they want to spend money, at times that suit them. Jane is verging on burnout. The financial rewards have been huge, but she has given up a lot in exchange. Mike, her husband, has taken on most of the burden of running the rest of their lives—their children are young and neither parent wanted to leave all of the care to a nanny. They have enjoyed their high income— and have certainly spent it! They live in a beautiful home, have expensive vehicles and are dressed to impress. The children have everything—except their mother. There is a great deal spent on takeaways, treats and outings to compensate. When the family manages to holiday away for a few days, no expense is spared but the holidays are almost as rushed as the work weeks. Jane is exhausted and Mike is fed up. Jane feels she cannot stop or the money will too. And they have become very used to living and spending at this level.

High income/lot of time

The only place you want to be on this chart is in the quadrant where you have *both* plenty of income and plenty of time. This is the point of being in business. This is why you took the risk of forsaking the security you left behind—a safe job, a steady income, a reasonable certainty about the future, however unappealing it may have seemed. Business is simply a means to an end. Yes, you hope to enjoy what you choose to do on the way through and yes, you may derive a lot of personal satisfaction from creating a business, watching it grow and making it successful. But a business exists to create wealth and to give you and your family a great life.

Con and Marise set up a software design and service business a decade ago. They both brought industry expertise and talent to the business, having worked in IT for major corporates before starting out on their own. They knew a lot about computers and systems and the Internet, but almost nothing about running a business. However, they were committed to learning and sought out good advice. They always dreamed of a life where they could spend time with the children, pursue hobbies and afford to contribute their time and skills to their favourite charity. Con and Marise sold down their shares two years ago to other people in their business. They left with a tidy lump sum (which they have invested in real estate with no borrowings), but have kept 25 per cent of the ownership. They have been retained as directors of the business, as their network and knowledge are valuable. They enjoy 'keeping their hand in', but no longer have the worry, risk or pressure of meeting urgent deadlines or taking care of many staff. Con and Marise spend a lot of time with their four children, are very involved in their children's schools and sport, and are learning Italian because they intend to spend a year living in Umbria very soon. With the proceeds of the sale invested and ongoing income from their share of the business, they have no money worries. In addition, they have time to live life on their terms well before the traditional 'retirement' years.

Take the time to do an analysis of your own situation. Write it down and make it real.

- What would you be doing if you had enough time and money—if you had financial freedom?
- What are the particular things you struggle with regarding time and money?
- Where do you fit in the diagram shown at the beginning of this section? Which quadrant do you belong in?
- How are you feeling? Are you worried all the time? Don't just focus on the business—the business is only *part* of your life.
- Do you have any time for yourself or do you suffer from 'temporal bankruptcy', even if your bank balance looks fine? How does this affect you?
- How much time did you work in the last week? Month? When did you last have a holiday?

- What is suffering—marriage, relationship, family, friends, health, social life, a sense of fun, your optimism for the future? What does your family complain to you about—or have they simply given up?
- What would be different if you were financially free? How would you live? What would you change?

Let's get to work on helping you achieve financial freedom.

Your wealth-creating asset

Businesses exist to create wealth. You own your business in order to become wealthy and free to live life as you choose. Owning and running a business takes a lot of time and commitment. It is also full of risk, so it is very important that you succeed. Business owners invest so much money, time and energy in their businesses that achieving anything less than wealth and freedom is unacceptable.

Your business is your wealth-creating asset. You set up a business with the objective of making money. Your business is the asset you will use to create wealth. Hopefully, it will give you a considerable income each year. Ideally, the business itself will become more valuable each year. This is not always the case: some businesses have little or no sale value. This may be because the business is simply a vehicle for self-employment, such as some form of consultancy; other businesses have little or no sale value because they are so easy to set up from scratch by a newcomer. Either way, your business is your wealth-creating asset.

A business is a machine for creating value. Your business should make you rich and, ultimately, free by creating wealth. The way you think about your business and the decisions you make should all be focused on wealth creation.

Your business can create wealth in two main ways:

1. It can concentrate capital value.
2. It can throw off a lot of cash.

And the best businesses do both!

Concentrating capital value means that the business becomes more and more valuable over time. Eventually, you will have something very valuable to sell. You will need to have an exit strategy and be prepared to sell down or sell out entirely. Many farming businesses concentrate capital value very well. Despite ups and downs in the market, farmland tends to appreciate well in value over longer periods of time. Many farmers, despite feeling poor all through their farming lives because of relatively low income, find themselves very wealthy when they come to sell. Many other businesses accumulate capital value by creating products or services so highly regarded that others are willing to pay a lot of money to take over that wealth-creating machine.

Some businesses throw off a lot of cash, even though there may be little or nothing to sell at the end. Many service businesses are in this category, as are many forms of advice and consulting. However, if the service is well conceived and well run, it can command high margins and owners can make very good money year to year.

Decide which type of business yours is. You need to either

create wealth by concentrating capital value in your business or make sure that you use the high income from your business to concentrate value elsewhere.

Some business owners are lucky enough to run a business that does both—delivers good profits *and* becomes highly valuable for sale. However, it should be obvious that it is completely unacceptable for your business to do neither. For your business to create wealth, it must deliver very good profits as you go or it must build up a lot of capital value for sale—and preferably both.

How is your business doing?

The wealth that you need for your future freedom is going to come from your business. You may be doing well already and have a good base to start driving up profits and growing the business. Or you may be struggling along—barely making a living for yourself and scrambling to make payroll for your staff. It may even be worse than that.

Either way, you need to spend some time working out where your business may need some tweaking or perhaps a makeover. Remember, what you are trying to do is create wealth—the business needs to provide lots of income (profits) or become steadily more valuable so you can sell it, or both of these. You need a healthy business to do that.

You know your business better than anyone else. The following health checks are not exhaustive. Rather, they are designed to help you see which part of your business is most in need of attention—in order to stem the rot or, more hopefully, to make the business better and stronger than before. Businesses vary enormously. Some of the checks below will be irrelevant to your business. Use your judgement. What you are looking for are prompts and clues about where to direct your attention. You can't do everything; you can't fix it all at once. However, you should be able to identify what needs the most attention in your business.

On the following pages are questions about major aspects of business. The questions are intended to help you focus on some of the 'vital signs'—indicators of the health of your business. There are not necessarily any 'right' answers. Rather, the questions should prompt you to look closely at the business and ask if all is well. If you don't have the information to answer all of the questions, then that is useful information in itself. The information should be somewhere and you need to find it. If you are not gathering lots of information about your business, you have no basis for making good decisions for the future.

VITAL SIGNS in ...

Finance:

- Are your sales trending up?

- Are your profits increasing?

- Are your margins increasing?

- Are your accounts receivable (debtors) increasing?

- Are debtors taking longer to pay than last year?

- Are your bad debts (write-offs) higher than last year?

- Are you spending more on administrative expenses?

- Are your unit costs above budget?

- Are you giving more credits than normal?

- Are you experiencing cash-flow problems?

Make a note of what needs attention.

VITAL SIGNS in ...

Staff:

- Are you having higher turnover of staff?

- Are you finding it harder to attract good staff?

- Are you having high absenteeism?

- Are you having performance problems with employees?

- Are you getting more employee complaints?

- Are your employees happy?

- Are you giving pay rises?

- Are you paying above average?

- Are you rewarding and recognising good performance?

- Are you a great employer?

Make a note of what needs attention.

VITAL SIGNS in ...

Operations:

- Are you getting more complaints from customers?

- Are you 'outperformed' by competitors?

- Are others benchmarking anything you do?

- Are you getting returns or having to issue credits for poor work?

- Are you experiencing out-of-stocks?

- Are your completion times getting longer?

- Are your fixed overheads going up?

- Are you as productive as the rest of your industry?

- Are you having quality problems like scrap, errors, rework, poor service?

- Are your safety incidents rising?

Make a note of what needs attention.

VITAL SIGNS in ...

Marketing and sales:

- Are your sales increasing?

- Are you able to keep putting your prices up?

- Are you offering something 'better'—convenience, speed, quality, service, value?

- Are you getting referrals?

- Are you getting good word of mouth?

- Are your products or services easy to find?

- Are your employees supportive of your products or services?

- Are you seen as a good local citizen?

- Are you supportive of the community?

- Are you the one to beat on *any* aspect of your business?

Make a note of what needs attention.

VITAL SIGNS in ...

Strategy:

- Are you clear about how your business makes money?

- Are you aware of any risks your business is facing?

- Are you taking steps to lower these risks?

- Are you clear about the next step for your business?

- Are you actively planning to raise profits?

- Are you planning for business growth?

- Are you clear where your business advantage lies?

- Are you decided on how you will win?

- Are you focused on the few key things you must do?

- Are your staff excited about what the business is going to do?

Make a note of what needs attention.

VITAL SIGNS in ...

Administration:

- Are you making credit checks before offering credit?

- Are you paying your bills on time?

- Are you actively managing debtors?

- Are your tax returns up to date?

- Are all policies, contracts, role descriptions and performance reviews up to date?

- Are all key processes and procedures documented?

- Are you legally compliant?

- Are you at risk from the poor handling of cash, banking, invoicing, stores?

- Are staff able to run their areas without your daily hand-holding?

- Are the important things monitored, measured and reported?

Make a note of what needs attention.

VITAL SIGNS in ...

Your personal life:

- Are you clear about your role?

- Are you following a plan for the year, month, week, day?

- Are you having at least one full day a week off?

- Are you getting holidays?

- Are you spending enough time with your family?

- Are your habits good for business—for example, exercise, nutrition, sleep, recreation?

- Are you reading about business, success and wealth creation?

- Are you networking with other businesspeople and community leaders?

- Are you developing yourself in any way?

- Are you feeling wonderful?

Make a note of what needs attention.

VITAL SIGNS in ...

Contribution:

- Are your skills adequate for this business?

- Are your skills, qualifications or expertise saleable?

- Is your leadership style appropriate?

- Is your energy focused in the right place?

- Is your vision exciting to others?

- Is your leadership attractive to staff, customers and clients?

- Are your relationships with suppliers and contractors good?

- Is your work ethic balanced?

- Are your character and ethical standards up to the needs of the business?

- Is your reputation good?

Make a note of what needs attention.

You should write down your answers to the questions raised in the 'vital signs' boxes. Writing helps keep us honest. It's there in black and white and it makes it hard to use 'weasel words' like 'pretty good', 'fine' and 'OK'. Some answers to the above questions might be 'yes', 'no', 'I don't know', 'I need to find out' or even 'Omigod—I never thought of that!' Be brutally honest with yourself—this is for you and you don't need to share it with anyone. On the other hand, you might want to discuss the results with someone who knows the business well. A business partner, employee or spouse could answer the questions independently and you could compare your audits.

The point here is not to beat yourself up or get depressed. Your business needs to fire in order for you to become wealthy and free. This audit should give you a sense of the key things that you need to address in your business to tighten it up and get it to produce the wealth that you need to set you free. Better business practice will achieve this in two ways:

1. Running your business more efficiently will give you increased income and profit. You can use this to reinvest in the business or divert into security assets in order to secure wealth away from the risks of business and provide passive income that you do not have to work for.
2. A business that is better run becomes more valuable. The business will be worth more when you come to sell if it has been well run for several years.

The next step is to look at the bigger picture of your business model.

2

Is your business model sound?

Your strategy for wealth and freedom

People who become rich and free through owning a business usually follow one of three strategies:

1. Develop a valuable business and sell it.
2. Develop a business that can deliver profits without you.
3. Develop a business that generates big cash flows and suck them out.

Develop a valuable business and sell it

The strategy here is to build a sound business with a view to someone buying you out in the future. You will, of course, want to make good profits along the way (so the business can pay you a salary and dividends), but you will also want to create a lot of goodwill. Goodwill is the 'extra' that a buyer will be willing to pay for your business rather than starting from scratch in competition with you or having to go through the same learning curve. Goodwill may be created through your reputation, your great team, your loyal customers, your wonderful locations and many other intangibles (see Chapter 6). It is the premium that you get from goodwill that will make you wealthy.

Petra developed her design and printing business from a small start. Over the years, she accumulated a long list of clients owing to her high standards of design and professional operations and delivery. She reinvested heavily in the business—there was little choice, as technology advances meant that her equipment became rapidly obsolete. The market continued to change as people demanded ever higher levels of design. Many businesses wanted short print runs that could be met with new and fast digital copying. Petra expanded her operation into nearby towns, so ended up managing several staff over a wide geographical location. Her business reputation, or brand, was very good and competitors would have needed to make a very big investment to compete head-on where she was already established. There are high barriers to entry in that industry, as there is considerable capital investment in plant and equipment as well as skilled labour.

One of the big names in the industry made Petra an offer she couldn't refuse—they wanted to dominate that territory and she was in the way. They judged it far easier to buy her out than invest the several years of effort and investment it would take to grab her market share. Petra is now 'retired' (read travelling, thinking of starting another business, playing with her grandchildren) with enough wealth to live the life of her dreams.

Develop a business that can deliver profits without you

This strategy requires you to develop a business that is large and successful enough that you can install professional management to operate it while you go off to live the life of your dreams. You may still be the full owner or may have sold down some of your shareholding. Some owners like to stay involved as an executive director or as chairman of the board. You can do whatever you wish—it is still mostly your business. However, the point is that you don't have to be involved in any very active way unless you want to. You will have grown the business to a point where it can afford good managers and it can run very profitably without you.

Alex's contracting business started off very small—just Alex, his dad and a lorry. Over the years, Alex added staff, more lorries and other heavy machinery. Alex's dad died and Alex was left with the business. Despite some lean years when the building market was slow and there was little investment in infrastructure, Alex survived and was well positioned when the markets recovered and the boom years arrived for contractors. Alex always harboured dreams of a different lifestyle—much different from 12-hour days, working in all weathers with frequent callouts over the weekends and holidays to deal with road slips, flood damage and all the rest of it. Sam, his son, has been involved in the business from an early age.

Alex has ensured that Sam has been developed well over the years. He received no favours as the boss's son; in fact, he has done every job in the business from the bottom up. He has earned the respect of his fellow workers for that and is well on the way to understanding how every aspect of the business is run. Sam, however, is still only 25 and, in Alex's opinion, too young and inexperienced in management to take over. In the meantime, Alex has hired an experienced contracting manager, Max, to lead the business while he takes a back seat and Sam develops his management and leadership skills. While there is a significant salary to cover for Max, Alex believes that it is well worthwhile to give Sam these years of freedom while he is still in the prime of life. Alex is still involved as chairman and owner, but this requires little of his time.

Develop a business that generates big cash flows and suck them out

Many businesses are not saleable at a big price and never will be. Most consulting and advisory businesses fall into this category. You can still become wealthy and free, but it will not be through an eventual sale. These types of businesses are very good at generating high fees and usually have relatively low costs—little infrastructure or fixed costs. The strategy to follow here is to focus on being able to get very good levels of income along the way and to take this money out and invest it elsewhere as you go.

If you are not already following a clear strategy to achieve wealth and freedom through your business, you should choose whichever of the three strategies above best suits your business. In my experience, business owners seldom become wealthy by chance: the smart ones have a clear strategy to create the wealth that will eventually set them free.

Michelle is a freelance marketing consultant. She honed her skills in the usual way—working for a variety of businesses, including spells at an advertising agency and near the top of the marketing department at a nationally recognised consumer goods firm. She now works from a small office where she employs a full-time marketing assistant/PA. She has good associates she can recommend for projects outside her field when that is what her clients need. These associate arrangements are informal: no commissions are paid. Sometimes she receives referrals from these associates too.

Michelle considered building up a marketing consulting business for sale, but realised that unless it became quite large, with lots of staff, and created a well-established brand, there would not be anything to sell in the end. After a few false starts and some disappointing experiments partnering other consultants, she decided to go it alone. She is busy and can command a high hourly rate as she is well known in the industry from previous roles and award-winning work.

Michelle understands that the high fees she gets are probably all she will ever receive financially for her skills. She knows that she needs to use this money well and has engaged an adviser to ensure that she follows a sound investment plan. Her business is a great vehicle for creating cash, but she knows that there will be little of value to sell when she is ready to stop. In the meantime, she is focused on building up wealth outside the business. To date, she has accumulated a healthy property portfolio and a good spread of shares. She is confident that she will be financially free by 45.

If your business does not deliver on one of the three strategies outlined above, you should get out: you are fishing in a dry ditch and your money and energy would be better invested elsewhere.

Are you fishing in a dry ditch?

Is the business thriving? Or are you just surviving—or even slipping below the surface? Does your business have the potential to follow one of the three strategies for wealth creation?

Can the business make good money? Sometimes it's not your fault. You may have unwittingly entered an industry or a business that will always struggle to make money. It does not pay to fish for business profits in a dry ditch. Have a good hard think about the industry you are in. Is it a profitable industry? Are margins good? Are other people making good money? Is the industry very volatile or cyclical, like farming? If the answers are not to your liking, you may want to take your skills, energy and effort somewhere else. Business skills are highly transferable.

Sometimes the problem lies in the part of the industry you operate in. Take the motor industry. Undoubtedly, many businesses thrive in the automotive sector—selling new cars, selling used cars, operating good service station franchises. But some of the sector is squeezed tightly. Repairs and maintenance is a good example. Insurance companies force repair businesses to tender for business, cars are more reliable than ever, qualified staff are hard to find and keep and the consumer is demanding ever higher standards of service at no extra charge. In addition, there are high set-up costs. And lots of competition. People shop around and buy on price. This is a very hard business to differentiate yourself in so that you can charge a premium. You may find yourself working just for wages—and barely covering them. If this describes your situation, you will want to think about how you can vary your offer so that you are different from your competitors or better in some way that the customer values. Then you stand out from the crowd and get the 'right' to charge a higher price.

The part of the industry that makes money often keeps changing. Twenty years ago, IBM was the giant in the computer industry. At that time, computing was about mainframe computers that took up whole air-conditioned rooms in the businesses that were big enough to afford a computer. Then the personal computer arrived and Hewlett Packard, Digital and Compaq put them in every office and made a bundle for a while. A few years ago you would have paid thousands of dollars for a PC that was not as powerful as your mobile phone is today. And it didn't stop there. Now PCs are a commodity— we have classrooms of them. Some homes have two or three and you can get a set-up for less than a thousand dollars. Now the computer industry is all about software rather than hardware. We pay the big money to Microsoft, Sony and Sega for programs, music and games. Pity the person who does not see the changes coming in time. This concept is known as 'value migration'—the place where the money is made (value) shifts in the industry. Have you got stuck in the wrong place? Can you see a shift coming? Do you need to migrate upstream or down-stream in your industry?

Still other businesses have a high mortality rate. The

restaurant industry is one such. There is so much competition and there are so many things to get right—or wrong! In addition, it is a fashion industry—you can be doing just fine and then suddenly the fickle market moves on to the next 'hot' chef, location or cuisine. It is very tempting for people who love to cook or shop or make beautiful things to be gulled into thinking that they can make money by opening a gift shop or making and selling craft or serving food. We don't, unfortunately, get much business or financial education at school and therefore often think that something we like (such as food) or that others like (such as shopping) or that we are good at (such as making things or fixing things) is a sufficient basis for a business. Those things are necessary, but they are not sufficient to create a good business that can make money on a sustainable basis.

The message here is that you need to examine your business model carefully. If you are stuck in a poor position that does not have a good future, you might as well cut your losses and get out. If this analysis helps y what is currently wrong with your business, you may be able to 'morph' your business into something that has a better chance of creating wealth.

Ric had been running his car repair business for several years. Despite being well known in the industry and busy enough to keep several mechanics fully employed, he struggled to do any more than make ends meet. The industry is very competitive and customers shop around for price. The business essentially sells time and that is a difficult model to create wealth. In addition, margins are low—you have to be able to command high prices if you are to make money by selling time. Anything that goes wrong—absenteeism, illness, rework—blows the budget. Despite being very good at what he does and working very hard, Ric could see that this business model would never deliver wealth and freedom. After some considerable time spent strategising and discussing his model, Ric has started to sell reconditioned cars. This is a high-margin business and one that sits well alongside his other work. His business has the tools, space and skills to do the job and he can take advantage of the customer database he already has. Margins have greatly improved and the business is now showing steady profits.

Remember, this is all about the future you want and the life you want to lead. You can't afford to waste your life energies fishing in a dry ditch, trying to prove that your original choice was correct. I have seen lots of business owners do just that. Assume that your business model has problems—almost every business does. Find them. Assess what needs to be done to put you in a better position. Act like your own consultant—you know your industry and your business better than anyone. Face the truth. Your wealth and freedom are on the line.

Can your business create wealth?

My job is to help you create the wealth through your business that will let you have the freedom you want. So I have some more hard questions and demands.

First, show me the money!

Try to clarify exactly how money is made in your business. What do you do? How do you do it? How much money comes in? How much does it cost you to do whatever you do? How much is consumed within the business? Which parts of the business make money and which parts spend money? How much is left at the end as profits?

It can be very useful to draw this out on a sheet of paper or on a whiteboard. If you have others who can help you or who are knowledgeable about your business, it is a very helpful exercise to do as a group.

The diagram below shows a model for a business providing some form of consultancy, such as marketing, engineering, surveying, human resource, recruitment or other kinds of advice and expertise.

The business has to outlay a lot of time and effort to find clients to whom it can sell. It may have a great deal of skill and expertise, but this business is still selling time. Even when the business finds a prospective client or revisits an established client, there is time required for taking a brief and researching the concept. This may or may not be chargeable. The same thing applies with selling the concept to the client and there may be considerable rework at this point. The business then has to do the work. This may also involve implementing the work in the client's business—working with the client's own people or with external agencies or customers of the client. At this stage, the business can bill the client (it may be able to get staged or progress payments from the start, if it has a well-established relationship with the client) and, hopefully, will be paid in a timely fashion.

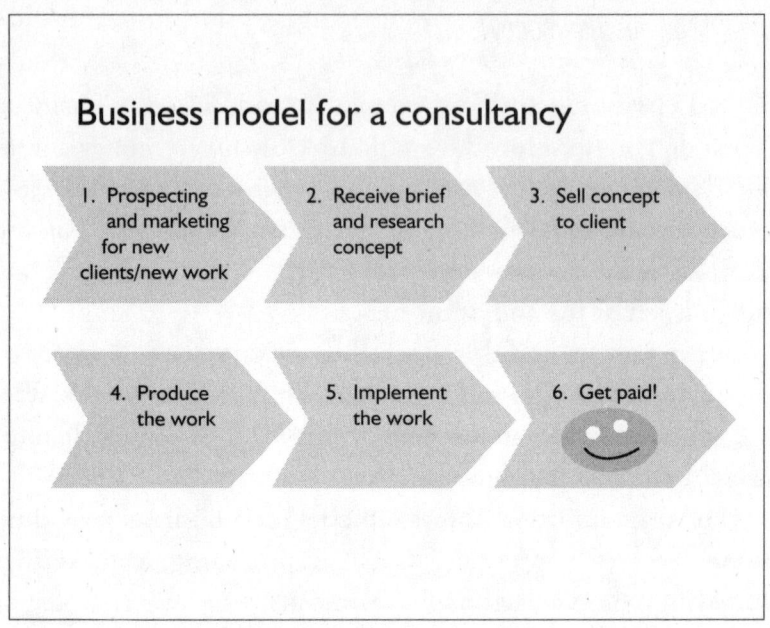

Business model for a consultancy

1. Prospecting and marketing for new clients/new work

2. Receive brief and research concept

3. Sell concept to client

4. Produce the work

5. Implement the work

6. Get paid!

The question the business owner has to address here is whether they can charge a high enough rate to cover all of the costs that appear in this model—time that is unbillable, travel, premises, doing work in advance of payment, and so on. Many people who are working for someone else see the big gap between what they are paid and what their employer charges out for their time. When they set up in business, they often overlook all of the costs that are in the business model and that must be covered out of the fees they charge.

A manufacturing business model will be even more complicated, as there are usually capital costs for plant and equipment, labour costs and distribution costs, as well as the marketing and operations costs illustrated above. Considerable amounts of money may be tied up in inventory and work in progress. Some owners' business models fail to take into account how long their cycle is; that is, how long it takes to move raw materials through the business, turn them into a completed product, get them sold and get paid. This model may be so long and expensive that it may be next to impossible to get customers to pay the high prices needed to cover it.

Draw a business model diagram like the one above to show how your business works. Ask yourself whether your business can make enough money based on what you think you can charge and what you know you will have to spend. You may need to have several attempts at capturing everything on your diagram and getting the numbers that you need.

Ask some hard questions about your business model:

- Are there lots of potential customers?
- Is the value of each sale high enough?
- Is it easy to get repeat business?
- Have you any advantage over your competitors?
- Are margins high enough?
- If you were not already in this business, would you enter it again?
- Does the wealth-creating recipe of your business look sound?
- Would you buy this business?

These are very challenging questions, but they are not an attempt to make you feel bad about what you are doing. Rather, we are trying to see if your business has the potential to make you wealthy and free before you go any further. Many business owners that I see feel a lot of shame because their business is not doing well. When we pull apart their business model, it is sometimes clear that no one could make good money in the industry—the model simply does not allow for enough wealth to be created. ·It is far better to understand where the problem is before you spend a lot more time and money trying to fix a business that may not be fixable in its present form.

Developing a stronger business model

Your business is a wealth-creating asset. Sometimes, when you look closely at how the business works, it may not have enough potential for creating value. Don't despair. Instead, start to look for ways to make the business better at creating wealth. Among the things I have seen businesses do to successfully generate more wealth in the business are:

- **Broaden the scope of the business**

Petra's printing business was ticking along quite nicely, but it wasn't making a lot of money. When we analysed Petra's model, it was obvious that the business was a bit of a revolving door: Petra and her employees had to spend a lot of time chasing down orders and often there was no repeat business, so the whole sequence had to start all over again. In addition, printing is very competitive, so it was hard to maintain margins. Petra was making a living, but it was hard to see how the business would make her wealthy. Petra then broadened the scope of her business by adding a design facility. This worked in a number of ways. The designers attracted clients that would never have come to the printing business and so fed the printing side. Work has increased, as usually when clients experience good design they start to review all of their printed materials. In addition, because the designs and plates are still in Petra's business, clients tend to go to her for repeat work. Design is not as price-sensitive as printing—it is more creative and more personal and therefore harder to shop for comparisons—so margins are higher. The synergy works in the other direction too: many printing customers are now easily persuaded that they should add a design (or redesign) element to their printing jobs. The business operates from a much more sustainable model and the higher profits generated by the new business model meant Petra got much more for her business when she sold it.

• **Focus the business**

Mike and Jacinta had a business importing frozen products for distribution to supermarkets, food manufacturers and restaurants. They traded in seafood, vegetables, fruit and occasional assignments of things that seemed like a good buy. They bought all over the world and had longstanding relationships with vendors everywhere these things were produced. Their model was very time-consuming and costly: they had to be across the markets in several fields, and margins on some of the products were very low. They had a huge number of stock-keeping items and their warehouse freezers were bulging. While they and their team worked very hard, they were making very little money—just covering wages and their own small salaries. This was no recipe for wealth and freedom and it seemed very unlikely that anyone would ever want to buy them out. After a lot of thought, Mike and Jacinta decided to focus on the fruit market. Margins were better and consumer demand was rising. Restaurants and food manufacturers were growing demand for top-quality fruit products and demand for organic fruits was almost insatiable. Narrowing the product range and focusing the business tightly in one area would allow them to use their expertise to grow their dominance in that area. It would also make better use of their facilities—they would be less likely to be out of stock if they had fewer lines of greater quantity and much of their distribution costs would disappear as they would be serving a narrower number of clients with bigger quantities. The business is much more profitable now—and Mike and Jacinta are paid properly for their efforts. In addition, they have built a reputation and a position in their market that should make them an attractive business for sale with some considerable goodwill.

• **Define the offer differently** I have mentioned several times already how it can be difficult to create wealth if you are simply selling time. The business is limited by the amount of time you can sell and there is seldom a saleable business when you want to stop.

Alf found himself in that position as a landscape designer. He was very creative and original, but found that no matter how hard he worked (or worked his team), it was difficult to create much value beyond a decent salary. With his skills he could have achieved that anywhere. He understood very quickly that his model needed to change. Over a period of time, Alf has added actual planting to his design business. Now his people come and implement the design, Alf can source the shrubs, plants, irrigation systems and garden features at very good prices and so can make a significant margin here. He has also developed maintenance contracts with most of his clients, so that his staff tend plants, mow lawns, monitor irrigation and replace any ailing greenery as needed. Alf has redefined his business from landscape design to worry-free gardens—he takes care of everything from A to Z. This new model is far more profitable and more robust, as it is selling much more than time. The ongoing contracts he has with hotels and major businesses, as well as with private homes, create a big barrier for competitors and make his business more valuable and saleable.

• **'Productise' your service**   Service businesses often end up selling only time. One of the solutions is to introduce proprietary products into the mix. Recruitment consultancies can sell psychological testing, trainers can sell particular branded training packages, hairdressers can use and up-sell expensive treatment products. It is worth considering if there is any aspect of what you offer that can be turned into a stand-alone product.

Maria's specialty as a human resource consultant was management training. She had a very good name in the industry and was in great demand, but her earnings were clearly limited by the days she could present and bill. She developed a range of products that related to her expertise but could be used—and bought—without her. These included skills tests, electronic training modules, management board games, and manuals. Her clients are eager to purchase these whenever she presents. They represent added value to the client. For Maria, these are a second stream of income and as the range has developed Maria has found further sales outside her client group. She is now providing electronic tutorials for offshore clients whom she has never met! This side of the business is very profitable and eminently saleable, whereas it is doubtful Maria could ever sell her consultancy despite her A-list clients.

• **Template your business** Many businesses don't work because they are too small or have only one outlet. You may need critical mass to make the model work. For example, one sandwich bar is unlikely to work well enough to make you rich, but a chain of Subways is a winner! You can spread marketing costs and the development of a brand across many stores. Your purchasing is far more cost-effective. Many businesses get stuck at the level of one outlet or remain too small because the owner is carrying the business in their head or has to be involved in every decision or every aspect of the business because the systems have never been documented—or worse, there are no systems at all. It can be very wasteful to run the business like this, as it takes very good people to run a business that isn't well organised. If there are no systems, policies, rules or procedures, you need the owner or other high-calibre people to make all these decisions. If the business systems are well pinned down and there are good routines, almost anyone can run it. My favourite example is McDonald's—a business with such good systems that it can be run by 15-year-olds! Needless to say, there are good managers in the background, but the point stands— the templates for running the business are in place and it makes it easy to open new outlets and to be efficient. A good template of how your business works allows you to get much better efficiencies in the running of your business and allows your senior people to concentrate on improvements rather than just keeping the wheels turning. Your business model may need you to be much bigger or to have several outlets in order to give you the scale to make you rich and free. You may need to start by developing systems that will allow the business to scale up.

Does the business pay you?

Owners of small businesses often try to fudge the numbers by working for nothing. And they are often doing the job of several people! The model does not work if the business cannot afford to pay you. This may be acceptable for a short period when you are starting out. However, I believe that you should at least give yourself a salary on paper, if only to do the numbers properly. And you should set a date at which the business should be paying an actual salary into your account. And if the business cannot meet that, you need to confront the awkward questions and have another look at it all.

Not only does the business need to pay you, but it should be paying you commensurate with your skills, time invested and level of the role. This is a complicated way of saying, 'Pay yourself properly!' For example, if you left a job where you were paid a salary package of $80 000, you need to be getting close to $80 000 out of your business or you are wasting your time. Every year that you don't earn this money is a year further away from wealth and freedom.

Your business should also be paying you enough in salary and drawings to compensate for the effort, risk and investment that you have made. You need to get a return on your capital as well as on your labour. We will return to this idea of return on investment (ROI), but for now you need to examine what you are being paid and whether it is enough. You need to be paid what you are worth. It is not in your interests to fool yourself about this. After all, your health, wealth and freedom are at stake.

- What are you worth on the open job market?
- What are you paid per hour now?
- What should you be paid per hour?
- What targets will you set for the short and medium term?
- Date it and make it happen.

You need to put the proper value on your time. That will help in focusing your attention on the most important parts of the business. It will also make you think about the hours you work. It will turn your attention to the prices you need to charge and, in turn, how good or how different you will need to be to

Value your time

Estimate where you should be ...

INCOME	TODAY	+ 1 YEAR	+ 3 YEARS
Before tax per annum	$	$	$
After tax per annum	$	$	$
Net per week	$	$	$
Net per hour	$	$	$

command those prices. In other words, valuing yourself very highly will prompt all sorts of other questions and decisions that are in the interest of your speedy journey to business success, wealth and freedom.

Valuing your time properly will make you very business-like about your business and your financial freedom.

What's your edge?

There is no point in competing if you have no edge or competitive advantage. This is business—if you are not competitive, don't compete. So what kind of edge do you have?

[handwritten annotations at top: "Time efficient - another one completed & guaranteed", "only female run buildings - business offering", "free project management & design service interior"]

This could vary from an innovative product to convenient location, to expertise, to superior service, to speed. Almost anything can give you a competitive edge. What you really don't want to do is exactly the same thing as everyone else. If that is the case, the only way you can compete is by cutting your prices and that is a fast way to business hell unless you have such huge volumes of business that you make it up in quantity. That is usually not a game that a smaller business can win and is best left to the purchasing and organisational prowess of the huge discounters, such as Kmart, or the fast food chains, such as McDonald's and KFC.

What are you really good at? Is it something that your market values? Could you be the best at it? You won't necessarily have to be the best in the world, or even the best in your class, but you will need to stand out in your area or from your immediate competition. Your service station could be the fastest or friendliest or most convenient, or have the best shop or be the most helpful in the general area. Similarly, your coffee shop could have the nicest staff, the fastest service or the best children's playbox, or be most friendly to senior citizens. None of these is earth-shattering to organise, but may make a very big difference to your trade, turnover and profit.

You have to know the one or few things that your business can do extremely well. Then you must stay focused on them. Growing your wealth depends on your edge.

Areas in which you might have an edge include:

- product quality; ✓
- location;
- convenience;

personal service

- service; ✓
- customer care; ✓
- franchise;
- proprietary brands or processes; *And at
woven*
- after-sales service; and
- expertise. ✓

You need to know what you are able to do better or differently than the competition in order to win with your business. The things you choose to have an edge in have to be things that your customers or clients value. It is a great waste of effort and money to build difference in your business that the customer doesn't care about. But just doing the same as everyone else is unlikely to give you the advantage you need to create wealth and freedom through your business.

There's money in dirt

People gravitate to glamorous businesses. I have already mentioned the tendency to open restaurants or own small retail shops. The big money gets hooked unwisely into businesses like airlines or car racing. However, if you are prepared to do work that others don't like or won't do, there is often a killing to be made.

Waste management, cleaning and storage are obvious examples. While these types of business often lack glamour and status, the returns are often very high. Is there an opening for your business to refocus in an area that others are ignoring? There is often a lot of money left on the table if you are prepared to do what others will not. As I write, the business press is discussing the prospective listing of a business that supplies casual labour. Most of the recruitment industry gravitates to the top end, where the competition for the relatively few executive placements is fierce.

Similarly, I have seen businesses that corner a low-margin niche, such as cleaning, gardening or waste management, that is unlikely to attract too much competition. These versions of flying under the radar of your most obvious competitors can have very valuable pay-offs.

It is also worth considering all of the 'extra' streams of revenue that can be attached to your business at very little cost but from which you may be able to take most of the additional revenue straight to the bottom line. This extra money can accelerate you along the journey to wealth and freedom. Think about some of the less glamorous additions that you could bolt on to your business to add value for the customer and make you some easy money.

Examples that I have seen include:

- electricians and plumbers who remove and dispose of old appliances for a fee, saving customers the hassle of a trip to the dump or the recycling station;
- gardeners who remove branches, grass and other waste at a charge and who then recycle it as compost—for which they also charge;
- automotive workshops that also sell car accessories and gifts for car lovers—they have already paid for the premises and staff and are doing this as a convenience for customers, not as an attempt to challenge the big accessory retailers;

- carpet cleaners who have added furniture cleaning and protection from stains and carpet mites to their repertoire— they have already made the trip to your house; and
- recruitment consultants who will write up contracts of employment, job descriptions and offers of employment— all saving you the hassle and at an additional fee.

Money—and profit—is no respecter of glamour. Often there is a lot of value left on the table in your business. Look around at what you do and consider the needs of your clients and customers—are there products or services you could offer them that might easily bring additional income at little cost to you?

Signs to look out for

Good signs

Many of these are the opposite of the problems discussed above. Good signs include:

- **Strong sales** This is the best indicator that your business model 'has legs'. If people are willing to buy what you are offering, and especially if you can get them to return for more, then you should feel quite confident of your wealth-creation idea.
- **Being able to charge well and get higher margins for your product or service** Being cheap only works if your costs are a lot lower than your competitors'; otherwise, they will follow you down the price spiral and a price war will wear you out.

- **Offers to invest in your business, join you in partnership or loan you money**   When others are willing to put their reputation or their money on the line, it usually means they think you are doing a good job and will go from strength to strength. They want a bit of the action.
- **Finding it easy to get people to come and work with you**   This is another indicator that the marketplace sees you as an attractive proposition. The more senior the staff, the truer this is: people are very reluctant to have a failing business on their CV, as some of the bad reputation attaches to them.

Worrying signs

Worrying signs include:

- **Falling sales**   If your sales are stagnant or dropping, you should be concerned. Someone is meeting these needs (assuming there is a market demand for what you do) and their offer must be superior in some way.
- **Selling on price alone**   Some business owners only make sales when their prices are too low. This is an unsustainable position in anything other than the short term. Sales will not necessarily give you profits. If you feel that the only thing that is attractive about your business is price, you should be very worried unless your volumes are huge.
- **Losing good staff**   This is never a positive sign unless you are also attracting other top staff. There is always a market for good people and you should be concerned if they want to be somewhere else. It may be that they see the writing on

the wall for your business or that they believe it is making no progress or growth. Good people will usually choose to be where they can grow with an expanding business.

By now you should have a good feel for whether your business—your wealth-creating asset—is likely to be able to create the wealth that you need for your future freedom. Your business may need just a little polishing to fly, or it may need a major overhaul to give you any chance of achieving your dreams. You should make a written note at this point of the key things you need to address to ensure that your business can and will make money.

Time efficient Benefits using my company.
Experienced tradesmen, thus no time wasted.
Guaranteed fulfilled the sales.
Woman. - personal service.

3

Working *on* your business versus working *in* your business

What's your job?

'Everything!' you cry. 'The buck stops with me. The customers call *me*, the suppliers ring *me*, salespeople continually phone *me*, the clients complain to *me*, the staff ring *me* night and day. Everything that can go wrong ends up on *my* plate—and that's a lot of stuff most days . . .'

Businesses don't fail to thrive because the owners don't work hard enough. The owners do work hard. In fact, they usually overwork. The biggest problem is that they are often working hard on the wrong things. We need to get you focused and your business positioned so that it makes you lots of money and gives you the future you want. Let's start with you.

Your role is the most important one in the business. Do you have a position description? What, you ask, didn't you leave your previous employment just because you hated all that stuff? Well, you don't *have* to have a job description—you are the boss, the owner, the head honcho. However, it pays to think a lot about your role. And committing the key aspects to paper will make you think more deeply about your job.

You are the managing director as well as the owner. There may be several other people in your business or you may work on your own. Either way, you are ultimately responsible for everything—and it's your money (and possibly your home as well as your reputation) that's on the line. Being the managing director means that, as well as everything that you do today, you are also the controller of everything that gets done by everyone else today and tomorrow and the next day. In addition to doing and controlling in the short and medium term, you are also the conductor in charge of what will happen to the business over the longer term.

If you are like most other owners of small businesses, you are very busy every day trying to make a multitude of things happen. The danger in this is that the really important stuff that may not seem urgent today will be overlooked. So, from time to time you need to sit back and ask what needs to be done for the sustainable success of the business.

Depending on your business and your skill set, you may be more oriented towards Production, Operations, Finance or Marketing. However, you will have to oversee what is happening in each of these areas, whether or not you attend to the detail yourself. And, irrespective of your preferences, you *are* in Sales. More about that later.

However, your real job description is to work *on* the business rather than work *in* the business. You are unlikely to overlook working in the business—you are probably doing that 60 hours a week. However, working on the business is far more critical to your future wealth and freedom. Money is made in top-end strategy, not in bottom-end detail.

What are the key things that your business needs you to work on?

The DIY trap

You are probably good at what you do because you have a tendency to get up and get on with it. Entrepreneurs are usually good self-starters and like to pitch in and get the work done. This is often very necessary in a small business, especially at the start. The trap with this behaviour of doing it yourself (DIY) is that you may continue it long past its useful life. It has made you successful to this point, but it probably won't be enough to take you where you want to go in terms of business success and ultimate financial freedom.

In order to thrive, your business needs you to do the things that only you can do—develop the strategy, plan for the next stage, get profits up, grow the business, find and retain customers . . . As long as you continue to do too much of everything else, these things will be neglected. The problem with these very important issues is that they are never urgent until it is too late to do them. Ironically, the things that seem urgent today and are taking all of your time will seem far less important in future months and years.

So you will need some help in order to free yourself. The help could be in the form of staff—if you need them, you can't afford to do without them. Just as we discussed paying you, the business has little future if it cannot pay for the skills it needs. Depending on the size and stage you are at, full-time tenured staff may be out of the question. But there are several ways that you can leverage off others, including part-time help, fixed-term contractors or casual staffing. You could also consider contracting out some of the things you may be doing yourself, such as preparing GST returns, delivery and debtor management. Needs will vary, but the point is that you can't do everything yourself and pay attention to making your business strong and healthy. The key is for you to be doing the things that are most important to make the business flourish—and to make you wealthy and free.

You might also consider leveraging off other people's money. You could take on a shareholder who brought some complementary skills. Another might invest money as a silent partner, but this would at least buy you time and resources. You are far better to own 70 per cent of a profitable, growing and valuable business than 100 per cent of a stagnant and struggling one.

If you are well networked with other business owners, you may be able to free yourself up a little by sharing resources—staff, fulfilment, receiving calls and making appointments.

Most importantly, you need to buy yourself some time to focus on the key things that need to be addressed to make your business hum. So, let's have a look at what you are currently doing with your most precious resources—your time and energy.

Audit your time

There's no one to look over your shoulder anymore. However, even though the old boss is no longer looking, it's still a very good practice to take frequent audits of your own use of time. Just as with eating and drinking, we all have selective memories about our habits! Try to keep a record of what you are doing by the hour. The professionals who charge their time (for example, lawyers, engineers and accountants) are very good at this. Many of them report in six-minute periods for billing purposes. That may seem excessive to you, but the principle is the same. Time is money and in this case it's *your* money and *your* dreamed-of future. Keeping a record (preferably over several days or weeks) allows you to analyse how your time and energy are being expended. You will soon see the patterns. What is taking lots of time that is of low priority? What are you getting drawn into that should be handled by someone else? What recurrent problems are you experiencing with the quality of your products or services? What must be fixed both for its own sake, but also to free you up for higher priority and future-oriented issues?

Knowing how your time is being used gives you back some control. You have the data and you can see what must be addressed or changed. You will also be able to see how much or how little of your time is devoted to the future of the business—how much time you are spending *on* the business rather than firefighting *in* the business.

Hopefully, you are already beginning each week and each day with at least an outline plan of how you will spend your time. Your time audit will let you see whether you are able to keep to the plan. This is not an argument for inflexibility—the best of plans often have to change. But you may not be making a conscious change of plan—you may simply be constantly derailed by inappropriate tasks, unnecessary interruptions and low-priority activities.

Talking to Mark, he seemed to have a firm grip on the key things that needed attention in his business. He was able to talk very well about the areas of the business that needed attention and the results that he needed to create in each area. He also seemed to have a firm grasp of how he needed to go about this.

But nothing that mattered ever seemed to get done! After having several conversations with Mark over a number of weeks and watching how he behaved when we visited his business, we suggested that he complete an audit of his time.

> The results of the audit showed that, while Mark had good intentions each day and each week of dealing with the key issues facing his business, he actually spent his time on whatever came up. He was very easily distracted by any operational hiccups in his business, even though he had competent staff who were well able to handle problems. This was where he felt most comfortable—doing things he knew how to do. This was Mark's comfort zone and he fell back into it over and over again. Likewise, he exerted no control over incoming phone calls or emails—dealing with everything as it cropped up, whether or not it was important. We found that Mark was choking the development of his business by being busy all day with relatively unimportant things while failing to deal with the big issues that would make his business more profitable.

Doing a time audit is not something that you will need to do every day or every week forever. It is rather a consciousness-raising exercise that you should perform periodically to make sure that you are spending your time on the things that you have decided are the most important for your business success.

Make some copies of the following time audit table and review how you actually spend your time.

Make some decisions about what needs to change. You might:

• work on fixing problems *permanently* rather than just bandaiding;

Time audit

	PLAN TO DO	ACTUALLY DID
8.00		
9.00		
10.00		
11.00		
12.00		
1.00		
2.00		
3.00		
4.00		
5.00		
6.00		
7.00		
8.00		

- choose to protect your mornings from emails, phone calls and appointments unless absolutely essential;
- block out a two-hour period each day for working on a key aspect of your business; or
- plan for some rest and recreation each day to keep you in the shape that your business needs.

Zero-based thinking

Working on your business is much more about thinking than doing. Thinking is hard work, which is why most of us would rather get busy doing—anything—instead! However, the quality of your thinking will have the biggest impact on the development of your business. (And it is much easier to get others to do things for you than it is to find those who can think intelligently about your business!)

One smart way to think about your business is to start from zero. Assume that you were starting your business again today, knowing what you now know:

- What would you do differently?
- Are there things you are doing that you would not do if you had your time again?
- Do you have products or services that in retrospect are a mistake?
- Have you taken on people that you would not employ, given a second chance?
- Would you use this location? These premises?
- Have you engaged with particular customers or suppliers that you would not choose to work with, given your current experience?
- What about professional relationships with bankers, lawyers, accountants—do you wish you had chosen differently in retrospect?

On the one hand, these are very confronting questions. On the other hand, you already know the answers. The value of these questions is that the answers point to key things that you need to address in your business as quickly as possible.

These questions will often tell you clearly that major action is called for, such as:

- delete that product;
- fire that client;
- replace that supplier;
- get rid of that employee; or
- change that accountant.

You won't have got everything right the first time; don't compound the error by pussyfooting around. In the light of your analysis of what you would do knowing what you now know, take decisive action and move on.

Act like your own best business consultant: the stuff you now know is hard-won expertise. Take advantage of it (it was probably an expensive education!) and act decisively.

The vital few

It is a truism to say that not everything matters, but it is a very important truth for the success of your business. The most important job you have to do is to *think* your way through the bewildering array of things you could do, could spend time and money on, could give your attention to, and focus on the few things that will make your business a success. It is easy to get lost in all you hear and read about business, modern market trends and the things you feel you should do, but in every business there will be a few make-or-break issues—and they vary from business to business.

The easiest way to remember this is to think of the 80/20 rule. This rule (or Pareto's Analysis, to acknowledge the genius who discovered it) states that, generally speaking, 20 per cent of inputs account for 80 per cent of outputs. In other words, 80 per cent of most activity is a waste of time, as it accounts for only 20 per cent of results. You can see this play out in all kinds of ways—20 per cent of your customers probably account for 80 per cent of your profits. The other 80 per cent consume lots of the business's time and energy, but only make up 20 per cent of the profits. If you have staff, 20 per cent of them will account for 80 per cent of the strife. Eighty per cent of your business problems come from 20 per cent of the products, or customers, or employees or suppliers.

Now, this concept is particularly useful when applied to your priority planning. What are the vital few things that you need to attend to in order to get the bigger success you want? For example, rather than being buried in the detail of your operations, you might say that you needed to get results in three main areas:

1. attract clients;
2. do the work; and
3. get paid.

Such a list would focus many service businesses on the few key things that matter.

Similarly, you could have a vital few for your own effectiveness and productivity:

1. sleep—getting enough of it and ensuring it is good quality rest;
2. leisure and recreation—being in shape physically and mentally to do the job;

3. family time—nurturing time so you (and they) are in emotional shape; and
4. focused working time—which you'll never get without 1, 2 and 3 above!

And you can keep using this idea further—for example, the key measures you need to monitor in your particular business, such as:

1. telesales success rate;
2. average time per job; and
3. average margin per job.

You *can't* do everything and you can't focus on all of the little things you would like to. Not choosing what to focus on will almost certainly lead to failure. Others will choose for you and steal your time and energy. Your job is to do the hard work to decide on the vital few aspects of your business that deserve your attention.

You need to think very hard about what the few key things for your business are and then make sure that they get your relentless focus and attention. To achieve wealth and freedom, your business must be profitable and successful. You have to know what the vital things are to focus on. These can easily be turned into key performance indicators (KPIs) that you can monitor and measure daily, weekly or monthly. Some of the key indicators will be financial (for example, gross profit percentage), while others will be non-financial (for example, number of sales calls made daily, sales call conversion rate). The right dashboard of key performance indicators will vary from business to business:

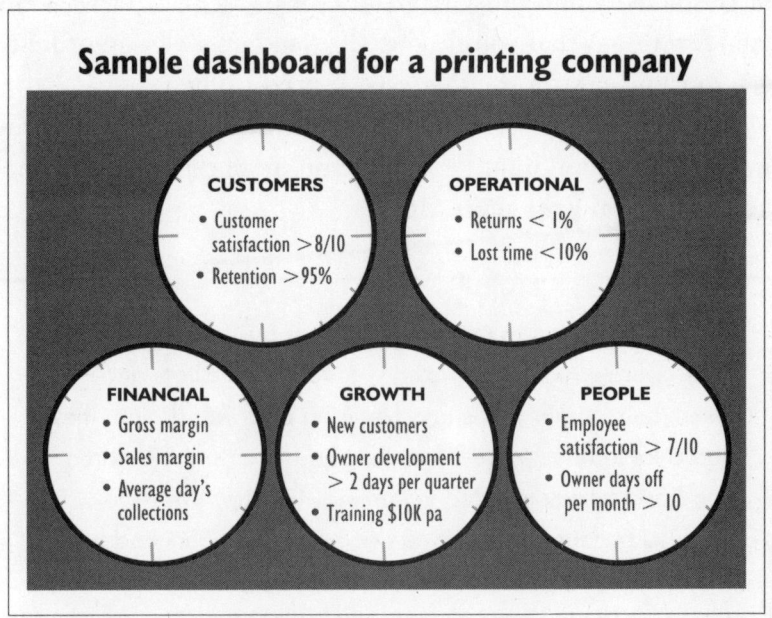

Are you doing the right things right?

Many business owners are overloaded because they are working too hard on the wrong things and neglecting the vital few. Over time, we take on more and more in both our work lives and our personal lives. We are much less able to delete things that are no longer important and that we should not be doing at all. We all know what happens to busy people—they get asked to do more things as they are usually seen to be high achievers. And you are probably inclined to say yes rather than no.

To compound the problem, you probably feel that you need to do many of these (unimportant) things very well—after all, you have high standards and high expectations of yourself. All of this activity and 'busyness' can crowd out your view of the vital few things that you need to do—and do well—in order to get your business in the state that it needs to be in.

You may find it useful to analyse the things you do, and the way you do them, in order to give you more clarity about what needs to be on your short list.

Andrew and Maria's marketing services business was frantic. They operated in a small town with few competitors and, given their backgrounds in advertising and web design, they had a lot to offer. In addition, they had three small children and had recently invested in home ownership. We were involved because, though working very long hours and with lots of business lined up, they felt that they were going nowhere. The business was not making much money and they seemed to be going around in circles. They had several ideas for new business streams, but had made no progress on any of them. Lately, they had experienced some worrying customer churn.

We did a time audit to see how they were spending their time and then analysed what they were doing. The results are shown below.

And that's just the work-related activity! Andrew and Maria were also running themselves ragged with school-based activities and new home projects. All of these are admirable and perhaps even pleasurable. However, the business needed much more focused attention from each of them. We worked on making sure that more of their time was devoted to doing the right things and doing them well enough to succeed. Much of the time needed for this had to come from dropping activities that were 'wrong' for what they were trying to achieve. Without this concentration, the business was unlikely ever to make them rich and free.

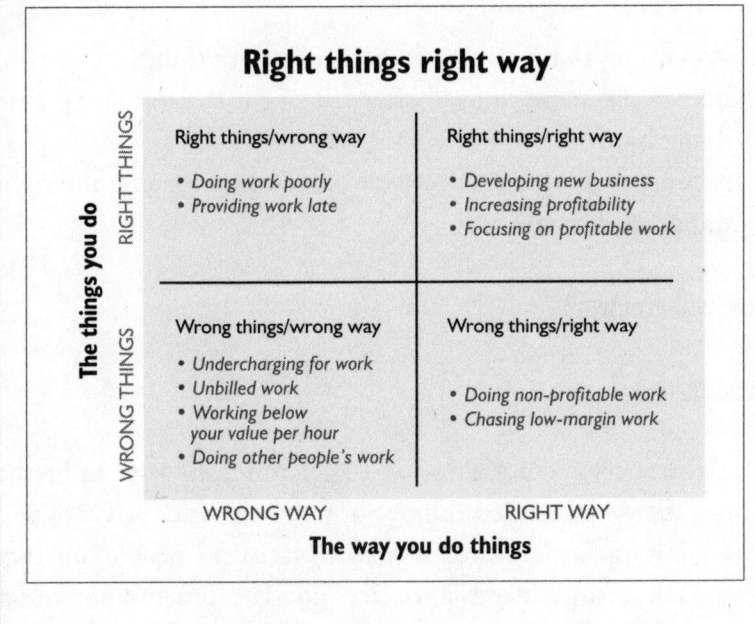

Right things right way

The things you do

RIGHT THINGS

Right things/wrong way
- *Doing work poorly*
- *Providing work late*

Right things/right way
- *Developing new business*
- *Increasing profitability*
- *Focusing on profitable work*

WRONG THINGS

Wrong things/wrong way
- *Undercharging for work*
- *Unbilled work*
- *Working below your value per hour*
- *Doing other people's work*

Wrong things/right way
- *Doing non-profitable work*
- *Chasing low-margin work*

WRONG WAY   RIGHT WAY

The way you do things

Working well on your business means that you are focused on the few things that really matter and that you do them the right way—giving them proper attention, dealing with them in a timely way, devoting the resources that are needed.

As you consider what changes working *on* your business might mean for your focus and attention, fill in your own version of the above table. Not only will you uncover things to stop doing, but most importantly you will identify vital things that require your time and full attention.

Consider what has to change so that you can give the key business issues the time and attention needed to make your business more profitable and ultimately more valuable. You may find that you can:

- stop doing some things altogether (wrong things);
- start doing some things better (the right things that you are doing badly); and
- become much more effective by focusing on doing the right things in the right way.

How will you win?

More thinking!

Every business needs a winning angle. You don't have to be the best in the world at everything, but you had better be very good at something. It's a crowded marketplace and people are very busy. Your business needs to be very good at something in order to get people to use your goods and services, pay you well, tell others about you and keep coming back. This is how your business will thrive. Do you know what your competitive advantage is or how you will win?

Right now, you may be lucky enough to have the only business of its kind in your location. That gives you a great advantage, as there is little choice if people want whatever you are selling—you have a monopoly. However, it will only be a matter of time until you have competition—and the better you do, the faster it will arrive.

What then? You could be cheaper. That may work for a while, but, unless you were price-gouging before, it may make your margins very low. The competitor will follow your price down—a price war—and then you can both lose margin and be poor together! Only the customer wins that game.

So how else can you stand out? Is your product or service innovative or new? Make the most of it before others follow you. It won't be new for long. Try to establish yourself, your levels of service and your loyal customer base in order to make it harder for a newcomer to eat your lunch.

If you are providing a me-too offering—for example, another coffee shop, another garage, another consultancy— think about the extra dimension that will make you a winner. Could it be your legendary service, your happy and enthusiastic staff, your incredibly convenient location, your hours of opening, your local standing, great network and place in the community?

Most small businesses do not have the luxury of inventing entirely new categories of business or of expensive brand advertising campaigns. However, you will be known for *something*. The more ordinary your business is, the more you will need to think about how to give yourself some advantage. And don't try to do everything. That will waste a lot of your resources. You need to do whatever it is you do well—and give people an additional reason not to see you as just the same product or service that they can get elsewhere.

Remember, this is all about driving your business—your wealth-creating asset—hard so that it produces good income for you along the way and becomes more and more valuable, so that you can eventually sell it and retire rich and free.

Now, let's look at getting your profits up.

4

Planning for better performance

Profits matter

The only thing that really matters for the success of your business is that you make good profits. Put another way, profits are the score—you make good consistent profits if you get the recipe right and you satisfy customers over and over again. Everything else that you worry about is a detail that contributes to your ability to make sustainable profits. You get rewarded in the short term by having your salary paid and hopefully by drawing big dividends. In the long run, you get a second reward, as others will pay you for this valuable stream of profits if and when you wish to sell your business.

Sales and growth matter, but profits matter even more. It is possible to have high sales or high growth but to be making little or no profit.

First of all, you need to think about your business profitability and about the returns you are getting on both your money and your time. This will give you better answers than merely looking at the Statement of Income that you and your accountant filed last year for tax purposes.

Return on equity

Your equity is the amount of money you have invested in your business. (There may be other shareholders, so the total equity may be more than just the money you have invested.) Not all businesses require much up-front investment of funds, but many do—for premises, equipment, set-up costs, vehicles and so on. Given the money you have invested in your business, are you getting a good return? It ought to be well in excess of the bank rate. After all, at the time of writing you can get 6 per cent just by depositing your money in the local bank and that is almost entirely risk free. (Banks are fairly reliable in this part of the world.) The risk-free rate that the bank is offering is your starting point for determining the rate of return you would expect in order to justify having your money tied up in your business. What return should you be getting? Well, there is no right answer, but the higher the better. Returns will vary by industry and by business—remember that some industries and some businesses are more likely to make good money than others. Business returns can be very high. I have worked with a small business that has achieved over 100 per cent year on year for a decade. They started very small, but they are very wealthy now—and all from a decidedly unglamorous business. I think it is fair to say that if you are getting less than 15 per cent on your money, it is probably not enough to compensate you for the risks that you are taking. And a rate of return much lower than 15 per cent per annum will probably be too low to make you wealthy and free in the time frame that you want.

If you have only started in business, it may take a little time to see a return. However, if you have been in business for some time, you should be quite concerned if you are getting little or no return on your invested money. If you are getting much less than 15 per cent, you should seriously question why you are carrying the risk and the worry for such low returns. You could have invested in someone else's business (shares) or made a killing on the property market during those years. Again, the intention is not to depress or frighten you but to encourage you to examine whether your business is doing its job for you—that is, making you wealthier. You should also ask yourself what you would need to do to get the returns up.

You can calculate return on equity by dividing the business earnings by the amount you have invested in the business:

$$\frac{Net\ profit}{\text{Shareholder equity}}$$

The earnings figure can be found on the Statement of Financial Performance (Profit and Loss) and the shareholders' equity figure on the Statement of Financial Performance (Balance Sheet).

Return on equity shows how well the business is creating wealth. *It is probably the most important ratio to the business owner.* If this ratio is high, your business is doing well at creating wealth—you will be making good profits and the business will be increasing in value. It pays to take your investment in the business seriously—you would be very serious about investing this amount of money in anything else, such as property or shares in another business. Much of your wealth is tied up in the business and you must get a good return on that money (return on equity) in order for you to become wealthy and free.

Rule of 72

One of the rules of thumb about investment is the rule of 72, which states that any compounded investment will have doubled when the interest rate (return) and the time in years have a product of 72. This means that if you divide the rate of return into 72, you will get the number of years it will take for your investment to double. Alternatively, if you know the number of years you are investing for, you can work out the rate of return you need to get for your investment to double.

For example, the rule of 72 shows that:

- $1000 invested for 6 years will need to get a return of 12 per cent in order to turn into $2000 (72 ÷ 6 = 12); or
- $1000 invested at 6 per cent will take 12 years to become $2000 (72 ÷ 6 = 12); or
- $1000 invested at 4 per cent will need 18 years to become $2000 (72 ÷ 4 = 18); or
- $1000 invested for 24 years will only need a rate of return of 3 per cent to become $2000 (72 ÷ 3 = 24).

So, in terms of your business you need to be asking whether you are getting a big enough return on your money. I suggested 15 per cent as a benchmark: your money invested doubles every 4.8 years if you get a 15 per cent return. It will take six years if the return drops to 12 per cent; it will take twelve years if the return drops to 6 per cent. The lower rates of return are likely to be too low in order to make you rich and free in a reasonable time frame.

Business owners should focus hard on the rate of return they are getting on the money they have invested. You need it to be high in order to create wealth.

Return on your time

While it's worrying to think of your money tied up in a business that is not giving you a good enough return, you should really be even more concerned about your time. As we have discussed already, you should be comparing the return on your time with the money you could expect to earn elsewhere.

Every year that you don't earn a proper income is that year's wealth forgone. You could have invested that money and taken yourself closer to the wealth and freedom that you crave. The business is your baby and you may tend to be very 'undemanding' of it. But while it may be close to your heart, you need to be tough-minded about your business profits (including your pay) or you won't be asking the hard questions that will prompt you to make the business better, stronger and more profitable.

Considering the return that you get on your time will make you treat that time as more precious. If you are worth $100 an hour as the managing director, you will be less likely to spend many of your hours doing $10 and $15 jobs. This is not because you are too important to do this work: it is because the business cannot afford you to do it. The business needs its $100 an hour owner to work on $100 an hour issues, such as customer development, profitability, and innovation of new products and services. And of course the more stressed you are the more likely you are to dive into urgent demands, fire-fighting and lower hourly rate work because it's easier than the hard work of thinking about how to make your business thrive. These distractions are your comfort zone because you know how to act and you have done these things many times.

You may find it easier to keep yourself on track by asking yourself if you would pay your hourly rate to someone else to do what you are about to do. If you would not, you probably should not be doing it. Delegate it if it must be done. If it is not essential (not a 'right thing'), don't do it at all.

Ask yourself again how much you are being paid and what hourly rate this represents for your efforts. Then consider what you should be paid. If you paid someone else a proper wage or salary for your job, what would you get them to do?

Business owners should focus hard on the rate of return they are getting on the time they have invested. You need it to be high in order to create wealth. Make sure that the business is paying you well for what you do. Make sure you are using your time well to grow the profitability and value of the business.

Now let's turn to some of the ways to raise your profits.

Sales are not profits

Because you work so hard to get sales, it is often tempting to celebrate when you are busy rather than look at the profitability of those sales.

You should start by examining all of your products and services to see exactly what profit is given by each. You may find that many of the things you offer are not worthwhile because the profits are low or non-existent. Many business owners lump all of their figures together in the belief that it saves time and makes things simple. However, it often means that you simply don't know which products and services are profitable and which are not. It pays to separate out different lines of business so that you can know—and manage—what is going on in each.

The worst scenario is when you are selling below your true costs. Occasionally, it may be acceptable to do this—supermarkets are always advertising 'loss-leaders' in order to get foot traffic, as people seldom go to the supermarket to buy one thing. However, what is more likely is that you are unaware that you are making little or no profit because the product or service has not been costed properly.

The first step is to understand your *real* costs. Many people, for example, complain at paying $30 for a fillet steak in a restaurant. They argue that they can buy a kilo for that and they only received 250 grams on the plate. However, the $30 has to pay for the premises and the staffing and also provide an acceptable margin!

If your business has become complicated and you have plant and people and several product or service lines, you will have a bit of work to do to figure out which things make a good profit and which do not. Your products and services will have an obvious cost in raw materials or time, but you will also need to allocate some proportion of your fixed costs (like rent and utilities) and of your administrative expenses.

The bottom line is that you need to know which of your sales are getting you good profits and which are not. The latter need to be fixed or finished altogether. The only exceptions are low-margin sales that you have to keep making in order to bring in more profitable sales.

Two figures really matter to the business owner: gross profit and net profit.

Gross profit

Calculate the gross profit (gross margin) on each product or service:

$$Gross\ profit = Sales - Cost\ of\ goods\ sold$$

For example, if you sell a product for $200 and it costs you $165 to provide, your gross profit is $35.

Your gross profit percentage is $35 \div 200 = 0.17 \times 100 = 17\%$. You should turn your gross profit figures into a percentage so that you can compare different products or services you supply.

The cost of goods sold is your direct expenses for sales—that is, the cost of the product and any wages or other costs directly involved in providing the product or service. It may well be that some of your products or services are giving you very little margin. This state often creeps up on a business as it grows unless you are doing the numbers and making comparisons all the time. Check to see if you can get the costs down on your lower margin lines—sometimes the business has become lazy with purchasing. Unless they are essential to your business, you should delete remaining low-margin lines as they are taking time and resources that could be better employed to create profits and wealth. Low margins can mean that you are underpricing, and you should check on your competitors. On the other hand, high margins can mean that you are overcharging, and may explain slow sales.

Margins *really* matter. If your business has a 50 per cent margin it generates $50 profit for a $100 sale. At a 40 per cent margin your business has to sell $125 to generate the same $50 profit; at a 30 per cent margin you must sell $166. Getting good margin is essential to both your profitability and the value of your business.

Net profit

Statements of Income can be very confusing but the basic business equation looks like this:

Sales

$$\frac{- \text{ Cost of goods sold}}{\text{Gross profit}}$$

$$\frac{- \text{ Expenses}}{\text{Net profit before tax}}$$

$$\frac{- \text{ Tax}}{\text{Net profit after tax}}$$

Your expenses are all of the other things you have to fund out of your gross profit/margin, such as rent, sales and marketing, wages and phones. These are the overheads of the business.

You can calculate your net profit percentage, or net margin, by dividing your net profit by sales and multiplying by 100. For example:

$$\$50\,000 \div \$300\,000 = 0.166 \times 100 = 16.6\%$$

Again, this number is incredibly important to the business owner. Is it high enough to compensate for the time and money invested and the risks you are taking? If the number is dropping, it should alert you to look for problems with rising costs, especially overheads, which can creep up if you are not vigilant. Cash flow problems are also likely if the number is low. In a period of growth, business owners are often so focused on a rising sales figure that they forget to keep an eye on their net profit percentage. Rising sales do not necessarily lift your profit percentages—in fact, you may have all sorts of cost problems associated with marketing, promotions, extra staff, more consumables, and so on. You should watch this number closely, as it tells you how your business is performing. You cannot become wealthy and ultimately free unless your business performs well for several years.

Get your prices up

Most small businesses have price fright. They charge too little to begin with and they fail to keep putting up their prices year after year. If you don't put your prices up each year (or more often!), your margins or profits are being steadily eroded by inflation each year. That's your money and you need it in order to become wealthy and free. So get into the habit of constantly reviewing your pricing and take every opportunity to keep it moving. You might want to diarise this for a twice-annual review if it is something that you tend to ignore.

You can be smart about this: rather than blanket price increases, take each product or service and re-evaluate it from scratch. You may be able to increase the prices of some items more than others. You may be able to make some minor (uncostly) changes to make something appear fresh and new and so disguise the price increase. Repackaging your offering in some way or reframing your services may make it easier to raise your prices.

It is worthwhile to continually test your pricing. Many owners believe that their marketplace is extremely price-sensitive, but that is often not the case. Look, for example, at how quickly people have become happy to spend $3–4 several times a day on coffee. You can buy a kilo of the best ground coffee for $30.

When you introduce something new, trial a higher price. You may be surprised. You can always lower the price, but you are giving away a lot of profit by beginning with a lower price if the market would have borne a higher one.

While I could never argue that you shouldn't listen to your customers, you should be very wary of taking grumbles and complaints about prices too seriously. Do remember, however, that buyers are liars. It doesn't really matter what they *say*— watch what they *do*. If you are losing customers on price, that is a different issue.

Address price rises smartly. Rather than put all of your prices up by 10 per cent, for example, approach each line item or each service individually. Some may be able to bear a large price increase; others may not. Customers tend to price-compare on some items (often basic products or services) but not on others. Continue to raise prices until you hit real resistance. And don't charge based on cost—the cost-plus method. Charge what the market will bear.

And beware of salespeople if you employ any. The first recourse of less-than-wonderful salespeople is to ask for lower prices, to make their job easier.

When you raise your prices, the additional income goes straight to the bottom line. Do the numbers: your gross profit (gross margin) will go up, as there is no increased cost of goods sold, and so too will your net profit (net margin), as there should be no increase in overheads either. You *might* lose some customers, but that loss is usually more than compensated for by the increase in profits.

The numbers can be startling. For example, a 1 per cent price increase might give your business increased profits of

$30 000. You not only get the profit, but you also have increased the value of the business. If we value your business for sale on its profits and apply a multiple of three (typical for a small business), your business is now worth $90 000 more than before the price increase.

If your strategy is to create wealth by driving your business for income, you now have an additional $2500 a month to invest—to add to the monies you already save or invest by automatic payment each month.

Price increases can be particularly important for people selling services or their time in one way or another. People selling time are limited by the number of hours that they can work. Putting up your prices means that you can earn far more from the same working week. If you have lots of work and your services are in demand, you should manage demand by putting your prices up—you only have a maximum of 40–50 hours a week to sell, so you should sell them at the highest price you can command.

Keep an eye on prices in your industry and in your area. Don't fall behind. There is no advantage in being cheaper unless you are attracting huge volume as a consequence. In the case of people selling time and expertise, lower prices are often seen as an indicator of inferiority. It is simply not in your interests either from a marketing or a financial point of view to be priced too low.

And keep doing the numbers: you may have to sell a lot more volume than you at first think in order to make up for lower prices. The numbers may also tell you that you can afford to lose some customers at a higher price point. Equally well, the numbers will show people selling services that their hourly rate is a very significant figure to manage in the quest for wealth and freedom.

Sack some customers

As mentioned earlier, you may find that most of your profits come from a small section of your client or customer list. It is common to find some version of the 80/20 rule working: you may be making 70, 80 or even 90 per cent of your profits from a relatively small percentage of your customers. It's a great idea to regularly order your customer list by profits and see how they rank and how many give you little or no profit (but probably lots of effort and difficulties).

Often, bigger customers may be relatively unprofitable, expecting big volume discounts and all kinds of extras. There's no obvious connection between size and profitability. This may make sense in your business: these customers may contribute a lot to overhead, keep your people busy at times that might otherwise be slow, and are sometimes the price for doing more profitable business with others. However, the point is to keep it under review. You might even end up turning away profitable customers and clients because your business is fully committed to unprofitable ones!

When you rank your customers by profit, you can ask yourself some further questions about the business relationship, including how often they purchase and how 'expensive' they are to do business with—that is, how much servicing they require and how much follow-up work is needed. Some customers are very high maintenance and you will want to review whether they are worth it.

Not all sales are good sales. Not all customers are good customers. If you do your analysis thoroughly, you may find that there are several customers that you should 'sack' or cease to pursue. It may have a very positive effect on your profits.

Again, you should do this regularly. There are often good reasons to take on a relatively unprofitable or difficult customer or client. But your business keeps changing and this situation should not continue unchallenged. The best way to do this is to have an annual review of your client list and see if you need a cull.

Reasons to fire customers might include:

- they complain often;
- they are poor payers;
- they haggle about everything;
- they don't buy enough;
- they only buy low-margin products or services;
- they are high maintenance; or
- their orders are very difficult to fulfil.

And the customers to consider firing are those who present several of the above problems!

Attack your costs

Costs are not nearly as important as sales and profits, and in fact most owners of small businesses are very good at keeping costs in check. However, it is a good discipline to constantly review your cost base—and to be seen to do it. Staff and suppliers, among others, need to see that you are focused in this area or there is likely to be a lot of slippage.

If you retail something or sell your time, you will find it reasonably easy to calculate how much it costs you to make a product or deliver a service to a customer. You probably keep a very close eye on things like cost of products you purchase or the expenses incurred in delivering a service.

Hidden costs are much more difficult to manage. If you have premises and staff, you may find a great deal of cost 'creep' in utilities (such as phone bills) and consumables (such as stationery and tearoom supplies). None of these are huge in themselves, but laxity in one area tends to spread to others and soon you'll feel like you have a huge new family that's eating you out of house and home.

Sales expenses are another area that easily gets out of control. If you have staff out of the office and spending money on travel, mobile phones, meals away and so on, you may find yourself racking up huge bills without the additional sales to cover them. If you are paying commission or selling through distributors, you will want to keep looking at whether you are getting good value—are you paying too much, making even good sales largely unprofitable? Or are you paying so little that you are wasting money by not attracting and keeping good sales agents?

Now, you do have to spend money to make money, but it's a good idea to keep costs under constant scrutiny. Review your suppliers annually and look for better terms if your volumes are increasing or you have a good track record as a steady and valued customer.

As much as is practicably possible, know what you spend on

everything. You don't need to do the administration or accounts yourself, but if you make a habit of signing all of the cheques you will soon have an intimate knowledge of where your costs are. Even better, you will quickly spot any anomalies. And everybody knows that you will notice, which is in itself a way to control costs.

If you employ staff, have very clear policies about travel and other expenses. Insist on receipts for all claimed expenses and query anything that looks unjustified or suspicious. This is not to make you look like a tightwad, but rather to be seen to manage the cost side of your business tightly. It will have the additional benefit of discouraging any poor or dishonest practices around your business, as people will expect that you will notice.

Catch that cash

Cash is king. Profits are necessary, but many smaller businesses run short of cash while being quite profitable on paper.

Many businesses extend terms of credit when there is no real need. If you don't have to, don't. Cash on delivery is a great system if you can make it work for you. The last thing you need is other businesses or customers making their money on the delay between receiving your goods and services and paying for them. You are not a bank and should not be funding their business.

Get money up front whenever you can. You may be able to ask for a deposit. You might not get it, but often that is the first, and very valuable, sign that the client isn't serious. If you go ahead and do the work anyway, you may not get paid at all!

At the very least, if you are doing big or protracted projects, make sure that you contract for progress payments. At the first sign of default on these terms, you need to take action. This may mean stopping work. The client won't be happy and you will need to handle the situation professionally. But you—and your profit statement—will be even less happy if you go ahead with the work and don't get paid. Many a small—and even large—business has been bankrupted by this kind of activity. Make sure it isn't yours. The more seriously you take the responsibility of getting cash in, the more likely you will be at the top of the queue for payments.

You can improve your cash flow, reduce your overdraft and drive up your profits by managing your debtors better. If you can't get cash on delivery, try for 7- or 10-day terms rather than the standard 30 days. Follow up quickly when you are not paid. Many businesses juggle their creditors; make it easier and most likely that they will choose to pay you first. Be ready to follow up with copies of outstanding invoices, phone calls and even visits until you get your money. You may lose the odd customer like this, but they will probably be the ones you need to fire anyway.

You might consider a minor inducement for early payment, but do be careful with this as you may simply be giving away margin. Consider other ways of getting people to part with their money, such as selling goods on lay-by and installing EFTPOS and credit card facilities.

If you have the staff resources, put someone in control of debtors. Give them the training and support needed and plenty of recognition for doing a good job. Debtor management is not as glamorous as front-end sales, but will be just as important to your profits. Customers who don't pay quickly have a bad habit of believing that they don't ever need to pay you! The longer you wait for payment, the lower your chances of ever seeing the money.

Cash is real. This is the money that funds your life and family and that will eventually set you free.

Stay simple

It can be very tempting to set your business up in style. But in the interests of your profits you should keep your business as lean and mean as you can. Buying buildings, taking on mortgages or leasing expensive premises are only the start. Many small businesses find themselves with several leased vehicles, office equipment and other embellishments that are not essential to their business at all. You know what you really need to get the business moving. Anything else is a cost that is eating into your bottom line.

So review your premises—do you need to own this building or should you sell and lease back? If you already lease, do you need as much space or as premium a location as you have? Do you have to have all those staff or all those office accoutrements? How many sheets of paper do you actually photocopy each month and do you really need that machine that is costing so much in paper, cartridges, maintenance and lease charges?

Unless something is essential to your business success, you should do without it. All these things swallow time and money—*your* time and money. Someone else is on their way to wealth and freedom by selling to you rather than the other way around. You are footing the bill and every wasted dollar you spend puts you further away from the life of your dreams.

You have to use your common sense in relation to expenses. Everyone's circumstances are different. For example, a coffee machine can seem like a great indulgence, but if it stops your staff from all disappearing downtown for an hour every day, it may well pay for itself very quickly. The message here is to be vigilant about what you are signing up to—make sure that your business does not have too heavy a burden to carry. A huge proportion of your sales each month goes to cover your costs. The higher your break-even point, the longer you wait to be in profit. In addition, if times turn bad, your business is much more vulnerable than one that is not carrying all this overhead and complexity.

Technology allows many businesses to be 'virtual' today. You may not need premises at all—a lot can be done from home. You may even be working 'with' others and all working from your respective homes. You can always meet in one home or in a coffee bar when you need to get together. Portable computers and good mobile telecommunications are cheap in comparison to offices and all of the costs that they entail. You can also experiment with 'virtual' staff—it is far better to spend a little more per hour for good people or for superior outsourced advice than to have the burden of full-time but inferior tenured staff.

Leave your ego—somewhere! Ego is a trap for your profits if you feel you need flash premises, a great car and all the trappings. It can be a particularly easy trap for someone who has been used to all of this ego-enhancing stuff in their previous job. The rule ought to be that you only spend money on the trimmings where it will have a direct benefit to the client or customer. I am far more impressed by the dentist's surgery full of gleaming state-of-the-art equipment and the latest technology than by the beautiful reception area and glossy (and, no doubt, high maintenance) secretary.

The simpler your business model, the less you own or lease and the fewer people you employ, the easier it will be to take most of your top line (sales) straight to the bottom line—net profit.

Making your business more profitable is critical to your plans to become wealthy and free. You can pay yourself a higher salary along the way and you can take more dividends from the business. You can then use this money to invest outside the business and build up other (passive) streams of income that will secure your future and assist you to stop working for money sometime in the future. In addition, a more profitable business is a more valuable one. When you are ready to sell down or sell out, the business will be valued on its earnings. The more profitable you make it, the more you will get for it when you sell some or all of it in the future.

The next thing to address is growth.

5

Identifying opportunities for growth

Growing your business

Businesses either go forwards or backwards—they hardly ever stay in the same place. Your business needs to continue to grow to stay healthy. Prospective buyers will also want to see a growing business with potential for further growth. And you need the additional profits that will come from growth to achieve your aim of becoming wealthy and making your time your own.

Growing your business means that you will need to sell more, so let's examine how you will get more customers, sell more of the same things or create new things to sell.

Are you good enough?

Your business has to be doing something right to have survived so far. But before you put a huge amount of resources—time and money—into trying to grow the business, you should sit back and have a very cool-headed look at your products and services.

Growing the business will require you to sell more. Now is a good time to see what needs to be added, deleted, changed, improved, modified and/or repackaged in your line-up.

Ask some of the hard questions:

- Are my products and services as good as or better than my competitors'?
- Do they perform as we say they will?
- Are my people competent at selling, installing and delivering my products and services?

- Is our after-sales service satisfactory?
- Is our quality high enough?
- Are we keeping up with customers' expectations?
- Are we good to deal with?
- Do we get referrals and good word-of-mouth advertising?

It's rather obvious what the right answers are. Wrong answers may indicate that you have problems to fix before you start trying to sell more to more people. It will be much easier to fix these now, before you create new levels of demand. Any problems that you currently have with products, staff, service and delivery quality will be magnified and exposed to even more public glare (and unhappiness) when you start to grow. So fix them now.

Ask for the order

Selling more to grow your business means that someone has to ask prospective customers and clients to buy! That may sound ever so obvious, but, like so many commonsense things, it is not so common. Many people who are involved in sales (and this may apply to you) would rather do anything than ask for the order. People hate rejection; if you never ask the prospective purchaser to buy, you will never have to hear a refusal. Salespeople much prefer to make calls and 'build relationships' than risk hearing 'No' by asking for a sale. Hearing a 'No' is good—at least it means you asked and at least you know where you stand and can stop wasting your time. It's best to get to 'Yes' or 'No' as quickly as possible.

Your success will stand or fall on the ability of the business (and everyone in it) to sell. Perhaps you are already very good at this yourself. Many entrepreneurs are; they usually begin by being quite excited by their offering and sell it enthusiastically to everyone. You may have great difficulty passing these skills on to your staff; they may not be quite as enthused by your business idea. Nor is it their house that is on the line—they don't have the level of desperation that probably has helped you overcome your sales reluctance many a time. Failure isn't an option for you.

On the other hand, you may be a very reluctant salesperson. Many business owners are. They set up their business to do something they like or are good at—like fixing cars, sorting out legal disputes, making cakes, grooming dogs, coaching children or providing alternative health therapies—but they never expected to have to sell! Somehow or other, customers were supposed to 'discover' them and come and plead to purchase the offering.

Many people feel that selling is somehow 'grubby' and that nice people don't sell. Nothing could be further from the truth. We are all selling our talents and our point of view from an early age. Watch a five-year-old negotiating with an adult. They have an objective, a strategy, persistence and no hesitation in asking for the order!

You have to overcome any tendency you may have to back off from asking people to buy. You are in a great position as the owner—people know it's your business and that position brings status and trust with it. You will also have to help your staff overcome any reluctance that they may have as well. Model the way for them. Praise them for helping people to buy. Help them see that it is customers who pay their wages. Help them to treat everyone like a customer—even if the prospective customer doesn't know yet that they are going to be a customer! The key is remembering that you are *helping people to buy*: people need your products and services and it is up to you to help them buy the benefits they will get from doing business with you. This is not a foot-in-the-door approach, but rather one that helps the customer choose what is right to meet their needs. Helping people to buy what is right for them is the start of a longer term relationship that hopefully makes you a trusted provider.

Selling is the ultimate skill. Cultivate that sales virus in your business. Reinforce it and reward it—and make it as contagious as possible.

Up-sell, cross-sell and re-sell

Before you explore any of the fancy ideas for growing your business, you should pay attention to the sales that are being left on the table right now. When you have a customer or client, you should always try to sell them more or something of higher quality (price and margin). This is very possible even with the smallest of purchases. Teenagers at McDonald's have no difficulty learning the mantras 'Would you like fries with that?' and 'Would you like a drink with your meal?' Yet how often are you tempted by the coffee bar owner to add a biscotti or a muffin to your coffee order? You are already captive—it would take almost no effort to double your order and ring up the additional sale.

Again, once you have decided to dine out, it shouldn't take a genius to get you to order extras with your meal, such as an entrée, additional vegetables, drinks, dessert, coffee—you are taking up the table anyway. No extra staff are required to serve any of this; almost all the extra purchase will go straight to the bottom line.

So think about what 'goes' with what in your business. If you print business cards, for example, can you get people to buy printed stationery, compliment slips, printed envelopes and so on as well? Can you cross-sell them to a complete redesign of their livery—everything from their business card to logo, to anything else they need to brand with their look? The design and printing parts of the business may be separate, but they can each cross-sell to the other.

Can you organise your business so that if someone purchases from you once you can keep selling to them again and again? For example, diarise them for further appointments, clean their windows every three months or put them on your schedule for regular garden maintenance.

None of these are difficult to do. Every business has something it can up-sell, cross-sell or re-sell. Your job is to work out how this can be done for your business and to teach it to your employees. These very simple and basic sales techniques are key to growing your business. At almost no additional costs to your business, they can multiply profits easily. All the hard work was done to get the customer or client in the first place. Now, with some smart work, you can grow the business this person does with you. The cost of each sale will go down, the profits will go up and in many businesses this can be almost limitless.

Use the growth matrix

When you are struggling to grow, it is a common trap to flail around looking for new business. Sometimes owners try to grow their business by attempting to do something very difficult, like invent new products and services to sell to new customers. You might be wildly successful, but it is a big gamble. It makes far more sense to look first at what you have to sell and your current customer base. A growth matrix allows you to examine the options in a structured way and ensures that key areas are not overlooked.

The matrix below allows you to analyse your products, services and markets in order to make considered decisions about how to proceed to grow your business.

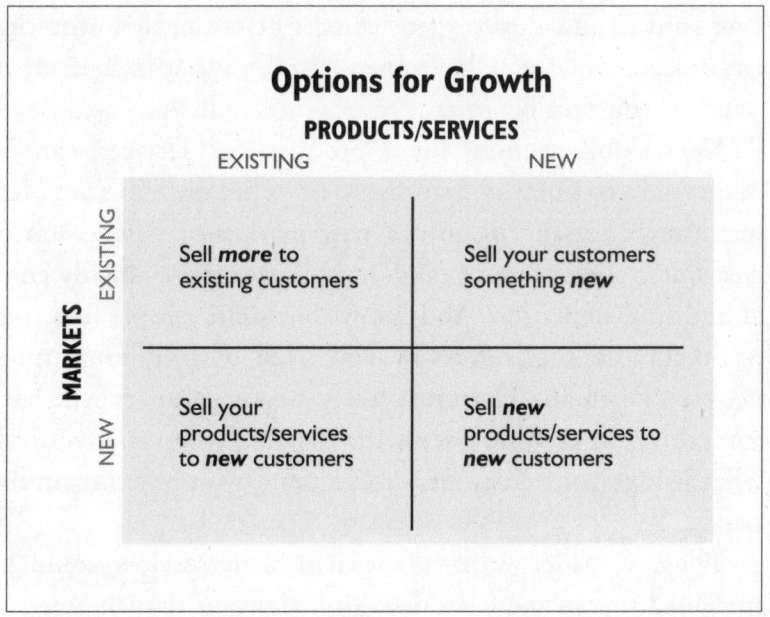

Options for Growth

PRODUCTS/SERVICES

	EXISTING	NEW
MARKETS EXISTING	Sell *more* to existing customers	Sell your customers something *new*
MARKETS NEW	Sell your products/services to *new* customers	Sell *new* products/services to *new* customers

You should start by compiling a list of your products or services (top left quadrant). How could you sell more of the same to your existing customers? Unless you have reached saturation point in your market, this is usually the easiest strategy and often reveals some very low-hanging fruit. Many of your customers could use more of what you have to offer. They may use only one of your products or services at present. Your job is to get them to buy more. You have the advantage of knowing these customers and they are used to you and like something that you already sell them. So think about how you can get them to buy more and use more. Can you move them from seeing their latte as a treat to having one every morning, for example? Could they turn to you for printed stationery for all occasions rather than just business cards? Could you cook for their family events rather than just own the local restaurant? The hardest and most expensive part of business is acquiring customers—once you have them, you want to sell them as much as you possibly can.

Next, look at how these products or services can be marketed to new customers or clients (bottom left quadrant). Expanding into a new market or new group of customers allows you to take the things you are already good at and find new users. You know that some people like your products and services. Now you need to find some more people like them. The most likely new customers will have something in common with the existing ones. Ask yourself what brings your customers to you and who else has similar needs.

Then, consider what new products or services could be marketed to existing customers (top right quadrant). You and your staff should know and understand the needs of these people very well—you are already selling to them and should have some idea about what else they want or need that you could supply.

Product or service expansion allows you to leverage your customer knowledge to find new ways of delighting people with whom you already have a very sound relationship. Increasing revenues from your existing customers is very cost-efficient: you already have these customers and don't have to invest heavily to sell them something new. They will be more willing to try new offerings from you than customers with whom you have no track record. Ask yourself what else they might be interested in, what problems they have that you could solve, what unmet needs you see when you visit their businesses. For example, a lawyer could discuss the relevant issues posed by new legislation, a printer might explore needs for high-resolution digital copying, a garden centre might try to find out what other gardening problems or aspirations the customer had.

Lastly—and this is where people often start!—consider what new offerings could be made to new markets (bottom right quadrant). This is high-risk territory where everything that can go wrong will. Ideas that end up in this quadrant need to be rigorously tested because you are in unknown territory—you neither understand this potential new customer nor have any experience with the new product or service.

On the next page is an example of how one particular business used the matrix. As you will see, the matrix provided several ideas to explore considerable increases in both sales and profits.

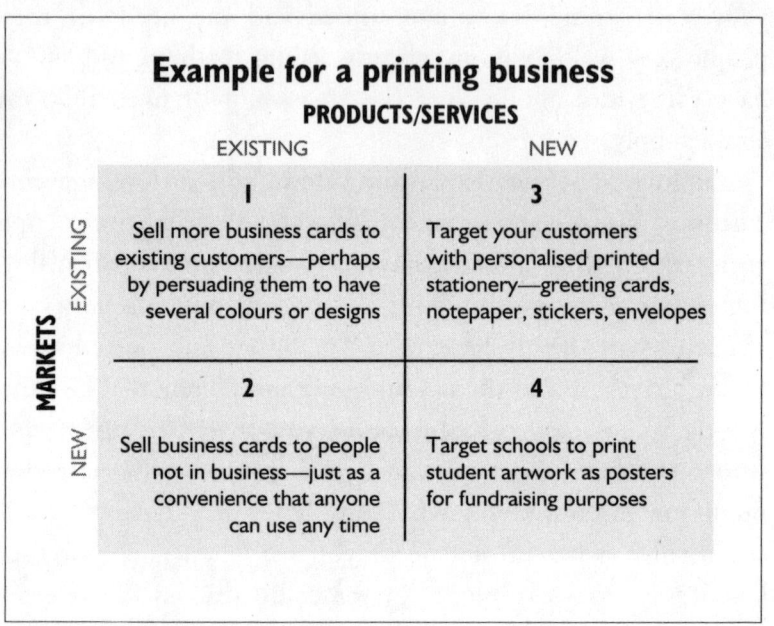

Example for a printing business

PRODUCTS/SERVICES

	EXISTING	NEW
MARKETS EXISTING	**1** Sell more business cards to existing customers—perhaps by persuading them to have several colours or designs	**3** Target your customers with personalised printed stationery—greeting cards, notepaper, stickers, envelopes
MARKETS NEW	**2** Sell business cards to people not in business—just as a convenience that anyone can use any time	**4** Target schools to print student artwork as posters for fundraising purposes

Your quote is a sales pitch

Many businesses operate in fields where it is normal practice to provide a quote. Most of the trades and many consultancy businesses quote on a daily basis. You should welcome the opportunity to quote, as it is far more than offering a price: it gives you the chance to make a great sales pitch.

Lots of quotes look more like an invoice. However, a quote that is truly pitching for a sale will spell out the features and benefits of what is being offered and will ask for the order. Your job is to help the prospective customer to buy: make it easy for them to choose you. It often helps to add a little urgency—for example, your quote might suggest that 'to ensure delivery for Christmas, we need your order by 30 November'.

Business owners often complain to me that they are under-quoted by inferior businesses. This can be especially true in the trades where, for example, inferior products or less skilled tradespeople may be used by the competition. The way to counter this is to supply quotes that clearly identify comparisons; you might, for example, show three prices in your quote, with each specifying the products and processes that will be used at different price points. Some people will still buy on price, but at least your better offerings will no longer be simply compared on price—you will have made it clear that your higher prices are justified by the products and processes that you use and the lower risk that you offer.

Painting quote

	VERSION 1	VERSION 2	VERSION 3
PREPARATION	Wipe down	Wash	Plaster touch-up
PAINT	Basic	Standard	Premium
NUMBER OF COATS	1	2	3
FINISHES	Walls only	Walls only	All trims
STAFF	Apprentices	Tradesperson	Supervised tradespeople
GUARANTEES	Standard contract	Standard contract	Money back offer
COST	$	$	$

You never know where your quote will end up, so present it in a way that does you proud and impresses as a sales pitch. Many quotations are barely more than a scribble on the back of an envelope. However, your professional, well-presented sales quote could be seen by several other key decision-makers that you might find it very hard to get in front of in any other way. Quotes to businesses often end up being delegated to a committee or may go well beyond the person who requested it, so if it's appropriate it can be a good idea to attach a CV or references.

A quote is often your first and final chance to sell—don't waste it.

Create a sales system

Good systems are everything in business. Unfortunately, we often think of systems for less important things like administration and never consider them critical to areas like sales and marketing. Sometimes, this may have to do with the types of people involved—back-office people tend to be systematic by nature, whereas many entrepreneurial and sales types seem to feel that systems will inhibit them. Not so.

Effective selling needs a system. Your sales system should have clarity around some key questions:

- What are you going to sell?
- Who are you targeting to sell it to?
- Who will do the selling?
- How will the selling be done?

- How will the product or service be delivered?
- What after-sales service will be required?
- Who will provide this service?
- What are the terms of payment?
- How will we be paid?
- How will we get referrals?

You and everyone else who is involved in any part of the sales process—and that's probably everyone in your business—need to be able to answer these questions. You haven't made any profit until the product or service has been delivered and paid for and the money is in the bank.

Many businesses never get beyond looking for likely customers and making calls or advertising to try to attract people to their premises and products. But you need to know how you are going to deliver on the total sales process in order to make profitable sales and to have any chance of getting the customer to come back for more.

Never forget that sales is a system.

Play the P's

You have to market your business in order to grow. Marketing can seem like an overwhelming field to the owner of a small business—all that jargon! However, the principles of marketing are very basic and don't change. Customers change and their needs change. In some ways, this is to the advantage of smaller businesses. You might not have the marketing and advertising budgets of the large corporates, but you are small

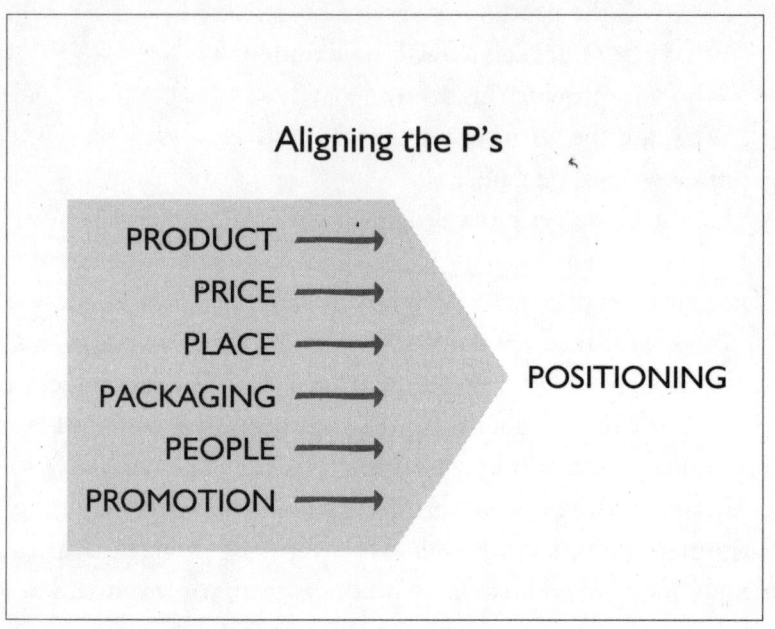

enough to be fast and that is far more important in today's business climate.

The most important thing to remember about marketing is that it is all about the customer. It is not about you, your business or your products and services. If you can hold on to that, you will never be too far off base. Keep the customer or client at the heart of everything that you do.

Then there are several elements you can play with, all conveniently starting with P—product, price, place, people, packaging and promotion. These will mean very different things in different industries and businesses, but they are all relevant in varying ways. They are all interrelated and need to be dealt with together; for example, you don't want to have a premium-priced product in a very ordinary package, or a premium service delivered by people who don't present well. In short, they need to be aligned—all of your P's should be sending the same overall message to the prospective customer. Together, your P's *position* your product or service in the mind of your customer. Your positioning is the result of all that you do. Make sure your offering is positioned exactly as you want it to be.

You don't need to be a marketing guru to look at your business under these headings and think about changes that could radically affect both your profitability and rate of growth.

Product or service

What do you sell? Be careful here. Many people describe their business in terms of the physical product they sell. The classic example that is often quoted is that Black & Decker used to sell power drills. But then they realised that customers didn't want a drill—they wanted a hole! Think about your business in that way. The garage owner may think they are in the business of selling petrol. However, the customer isn't really interested in petrol; rather, they are meeting their need for mobility and travel. If the garage owner starts to think in terms of meeting the needs of the travelling public, then the business—and what it sells and how it sells it—starts to look quite different. Take the drycleaners; people are actually purchasing good appearance. What else does this suggest that you might sell? Think in terms of the problem that you solve (lack of time, lack of skill) or the need that you meet (looking good, pleasure, status, convenience) or the difficulties that you remove (guilt, too much to do, not enough time at home, lack of leisure). In the case of the drycleaners, this might lead to marketing the cleaning of bedding, cleaning school uniforms over the weekend, maintaining upholstery, making small clothing repairs, providing an agency for larger repairs or selling accessories such as clothes hangers and garment bags.

Price

There is no right price. But it should be obvious by now that all of these P's need to be aligned; that is, they need to send consistent messages. Pricing does not get nearly enough attention in most businesses. Lazy people always sell on price and incompetent salespeople always blame pricing for their lack of success. However, you need to think carefully about your pricing policies. What will the market bear? Are you charging enough or unwittingly sending a message that you can't be very good? This is often the case with services where there is no tangible product to examine. Professionals are often judged by their hourly rate, so you do yourself no service by being cheap—it probably positions you as not being very good! You should charge as much as you possibly can without severely impacting on your sales. Keep doing the numbers. It may be in your interests to lose sales as long as the ones you keep pay the higher price. This is especially true when you are selling time; six billable hours at $100 per hour earns you more than eight hours at $70 an hour. In addition, it's a lot easier on the person doing the work and may mean that the work is much higher quality. Keep an eye on the pricing practices and payment models of other businesses—you may find some good ideas that you can copy and ways to improve your profitability.

Place

This is all about how your product is distributed and made available to your customer. Again, you need to think about what works for the customer and the messages you are sending. Take a large discounter like Kmart. You'd expect to find them in a shopping complex with a big basic store. The day that they open small outlets in high-priced high streets is the day you'll stop believing that they are offering a bargain. Likewise, you'd expect a high-priced professional who is targeting business clients to have a smart office downtown handy to their target market. Distribute your product in a way that is convenient for the customer and that meets their needs; for example, gardening centres need ample parking, plenty of trolleys and ideally a compound to hold the kids while customers make their selection. You do not have to do your own distribution, of course. Many businesses hand this over to other agencies that specialise in distribution, such as couriers, carriers or distribution warehouses. Trying to do everything yourself is often a disaster, as you will not be able to be good at all of your marketing P's and the ones you do poorly will let you down in the eyes of your customers. Think about how your product or service will get to your customer and arrange your distribution to match your overall position. Home delivery can seem very expensive but may not be—and often has the benefit of allowing you to target the customers you want on their own patch. Technology can be a great boon to the smaller business, as it is cheap and may help you avoid expensive premises or outlets. Consider a website and Internet sales. You will have to spend a little on arranging security for payment, but may make huge savings elsewhere. In addition, it may grow your business hugely, as you are no longer a captive of your geography—nobody knows or cares where you are as long as you can deliver. Your 'place' on the web is just as important as any physical location you have, so make sure it is sending the right message to your prospective clients.

People

Who is the prospective customer? Paint as vivid a picture of them as you can. Find out everything you can about these people. What do they do? How much do they earn? How do they live? What do they spend money on? What do they want? What problems have they got? What do they read? What influences them? The better you understand your likely customer, the better you can tailor everything you do to reach them and to be the answer to their needs or desires. Some business owners do this intuitively; others have to learn to put a lot of effort into this process. It is not enough to consider your own likes and dislikes, your own behaviour and preferences. The point here is that you need to stand in the shoes of—or better still, get inside the minds of—your prospective customers. Listen to what people say, but, even more importantly, watch what they do. Don't hide away in your business or workshop, even if that's what you really like to do. Hang out where your existing or desired customers congregate and study them—you cannot understand your customers too well.

Think about yourself and all of your staff who interface with clients. This includes any agencies or intermediaries that you use. Are they appropriate for the role? Do they mix well with the prospective customers? Are they acceptable to them? Who is very successful with these clients (perhaps someone from a competitor) and how is that done? Can you copy the strategy?

Have you got staff who like people and treat customers well? This is hard to teach people. It is easier, generally, to hire people who care for others and teach them the other skills they need. Business owners often make the mistake of hiring skilled people who are good at the technicalities of their job but who hate customers! This is not a winning formula.

Packaging

We all know that a picture is worth a thousand words and that so many of our judgements are based on appearances. This does not make us shallow; it simply means that we take in a great deal of information and messages through our eyes. Impressions count for a lot—even when we all agree that they should not. You must use these concepts to your advantage in your business. Think about packaging in the widest of terms—everything from your own appearance to that of your premises, to how you present your products, to the look of your promotional materials. Your packaging needs to reflect your positioning—the Mercedes showroom looks a lot different from the Skoda floor. You expect to see the owner of the gardening services business in overalls—it means he probably knows how to do the job you want to contract—but it would not impress you to find a $300 per hour barrister so attired. Consumer products are very good at this; house brands are usually in plain cheap packages to signal no frills value, whereas the strongest brands in each category have the glossiest packs with the most sophisticated advertisements and presentation. Alignment is the key idea: make sure everything lines up to send the message that you want and that will appeal to your potential customers.

Promotion

Many owners of small businesses think that promotion means advertising. Advertising is only one option and often a very difficult one because of the costs involved. Advertising can be very effective and worth the money, but can easily be a waste of time. It is estimated that at least half of all advertising expenditure is wasted, but the problem is that no one knows which half! You will need to choose your media carefully—advertising on TV will be beyond most small businesses. Local papers, local radio, trade journals, newsletters, billboards and the Internet offer more affordable options. Choose your placement carefully and monitor the effects so that you know what to keep doing and what to discontinue.

Direct mail and local mail drops can be very effective, particularly if you have seasonal offers or special promotions to communicate; for example, back-to-school, winter heating, home maintenance or new menus.

Sponsorship, if chosen carefully, executed well and leveraged properly, can represent a good use of your promotional dollar. Don't be gulled into just making contributions of hundreds of dollars to local events and persons; you need to decide what to associate with in order to best present your business and reach the people you want to communicate with.

Many of the things that work really well are very cheap, such as demonstrations (of catering, birthday cakes, new gadgets, household appliances, tools), open days (of factories, homes, resorts, schools, rest homes) and free seminars (legal issues, tax requirements, training needs, building techniques, gardening). Not only do they attract a crowd, but you also have a captive audience to market to and follow up afterwards. The more intangible your offering is, such as advice of some sort, the more important it is to build trust by letting people see you in action and by taking away some of their fears about approaching you.

You should ensure that there is a promotional calendar for the year—what promotions you are going to undertake and when. This should be planned and budgeted for well in advance. Many businesses never think about promotion until sales flag and then they spend money in a panic, often unwisely. Marketing well and consistently will grow your business.

Positioning

As the name suggests, positioning is about how you position your business relative to your competition. Ask yourself—and preferably some others as well—how you are seen relative to other offerings that you compete with. The two main dimensions are probably around quality and price.

Consistency is important. It is very difficult to market products and services that are all over the place, where some aspects of what you do are high-quality and others are low-quality. Businesses that have low-price, lower quality offerings often separate these from their high-end offerings to avoid pollution. You can do this by appearing to be two separate businesses or having different premises, or some such device.

The point is that it is very difficult for the customer to reconcile you mixing them up; for example, a high-priced restaurant with white tablecloths that is operating a takeaway out the side. So think carefully about which segment your product or service should appeal to and what that customer needs. Then you can make sure that your product delivers the qualities that are needed—speed, convenience, high performance, durability, reliability, appearance—and you can market those qualities in all of your promotions and communications. And then you must deliver. It will be fatal to your business to try to create one position in the customer's mind and then to give them an experience that does not live up to your promise. Businesses like McDonald's excel because they deliver exactly what they promise—inexpensive food fast every time. They never lead you to expect silver service and they never charge you silver service prices. Their position is very clear and they never do anything to confuse that positioning.

Ask yourself where your business is currently positioned and where it should be positioned for greater growth and health. Then get busy making the changes needed.

Getting all your P's in a line, so that they send the message your customers need to hear, is critical to continuing to grow your business—profitably!

Get referrals

Your business will grow if you can get more people to buy more. By far the best and cheapest way to achieve this is to get referrals from existing happy customers. If you say that you are wonderful, you are unlikely to be believed; if friends and associates say that you are good to deal with, the door is open for you to do new business with new clients. People trust neighbours, friends and colleagues about their experiences, and you come under the mantle of that trust if you can get referrals.

Always ask for referrals. You can be explicit: 'Who else do you know that we could help with this?' You can make it easy for people to refer you on: 'Here's another (sample product, business card, ticket) for you to give to a friend'.

Word-of-mouth advertising is the best kind of all—and no amount of money will buy it. Think about low-cost things that you can do that will wow your customers and make it likely that they will tell others. The prospective clients will be impressed and your customer gets the kudos of being the one smart enough to find you in the first place. Going the extra mile makes a big impression; for example, the drycleaner who stayed open late to allow you to pick up your suit, the dentist who called to see if you had any residual pain, the person who delivered something home to you at no extra charge.

Satisfied clients are often flattered to be asked to be a referee for you—and will say things about you that you couldn't possibly claim yourself. Make sure that you thank people for this. On the other hand, you shouldn't offer (or take) any commission for such referrals—they no longer have any ring of truth and the referee is now involved in the transaction. It is perfectly appropriate for businesses to refer to each other—the seller of shoes might well recommend the local cobbler for appropriate shoe care, and vice versa for expertise in fitting and sourcing footwear, but it is a mistake to put these referrals on a monetary basis.

Ask yourself: 'Would I recommend me?' If not, figure out what you need to do to make yourself and your business referable. If you can get good people saying good things about your products and services, you will have to beat the new customers from your door. What joy!

Borrow ideas

Originality is vastly overrated! There are enough good ideas in the world to keep us all busy forever without ever coming up with a new one. Many owners of small businesses worry that they are not 'creative' enough to grow the business, that they do not have the marketing 'genius' to come up with novel ideas and that they are not sufficiently 'entrepreneurial' to be a resounding success. This is *not* true!

Brilliant ideas abound everywhere. You see good examples of great business practices every day everywhere you look— and also evidence of stuff that you know you must *never* do in your business. Think of all the great—and appalling— experiences you have had as a client and customer. You could spend the rest of your life just implementing the things you already 'know' would be good for your business. Don't torture yourself trying to dream up things that have never been done before; instead, focus on what works. Look around at what is tried and true in other businesses and industries and see what you can borrow that would be good for your business growth and profitability.

The trick here is to become a magpie—keep your eyes and ears open and pick up as many ideas as you can to apply to your business. The jargon for this is 'benchmarking'. The idea is to seek out best practice elsewhere and then see how it can be applied to your business. For example, if there is a distribution component in your business, you might ask why if Federal Express can send anything anywhere in the world in three days it takes a fortnight for you to deliver firewood five kilometres away. You may not want to match Fedex (and your customers might not be willing to pay the extra costs), but at least it will spur you to think about what you do and how you do it and make you question your time frames and your distribution set-up.

You don't need to be original, you only need to apply good ideas. The most basic ideas reworked make for very good business. Find the good practices all around you and see if you can apply them to your business. They will give you an edge, if only temporarily. Others will follow you and match your offer, so you have to be on the hunt for new ideas constantly.

Take every opportunity you can to look at other businesses. Don't restrict yourself to your own industry or even small business. One of the disadvantages many business owners have is that they have never worked in a truly great business. Getting inside businesses that exemplify best practice in some area— for example, sales, marketing, manufacturing, distribution, operations, customer service or debtor management—will give you a wealth of ideas to rework in your own business. You are not in competition with big business and many of them will freely share what they do. You can also achieve this effect by reading widely.

Start looking—you'll find good ideas in the most surprising places. There is always a better way and the true businessperson will find it.

Watch the competition

It is all too easy to become obsessed with your rivals and let that blind you to everything else. Certainly, you have to keep an eye on them, but not to the extent that it prevents you from playing your own game. And some of the best ideas for your growth and profitability will not be found in your own sphere of competition but in businesses that don't seem at all related to yours.

However, that is not to say that you should not run your eye over your direct competitors often. What are they doing? Who are they targeting? What do customers say? Are you taking theirs or are they poaching yours? What do they do better?

You can do some competitive analysis, as shown below.

Beware of defining your competition too narrowly. For example, your products or services might target children in some way, such as selling educational toys or books. Your competitors are not just those businesses that sell similar stuff but every other business targeting the discretionary dollar spent on children: entertainment (such as movies, rental videos, video games and games arcades), other treats, (such as McDonald's, ice-cream and toys), outings (such as visits to entertainment parks and zoos), equipment (such as DVD players and video game consoles). Again, the idea is not to overwhelm you but to encourage you to look widely at the competition and see what you can usefully copy. It also encourages you to keep up with

Competitive analysis form

	My business	Competitor 1	Competitor 2	Competitor 3
Fees				
Image/reputation				
Market strategy				
Niche				
Quality				
Client buying considerations				
Other				
Other				

where your customer base is at and offer them matching 'value' for their spend or something different that is attractive to them (and their parents!).

Do your best to understand your competition and where your business sits relative to them. If you understand the competition well, you should be able to predict what they will do next. Try to write their plan for the coming year. What should your competitive response be to that plan?

And if you don't have any direct competitors, you ought to invent one! Seriously, imagine what a really good competitor could be doing to undermine your success. You know better than anyone what could be done to challenge you and where your weaknesses are. An imaginary competitor can be as good as a real one to help you focus on what you need to do. The golden rule is not to overestimate the competition. Don't underestimate them either.

Build a network

People often associate networking with 'greasing' and politicking—something that, just like selling, isn't very nice. Get over it. Whatever it is that you do, people need to know about it and know you so that they can buy from you. The more people you know, the better connected you are, the easier it is for people to access what you sell, to know and trust you, and to think of you whenever they have a need that you could meet. All of this assumes that you have something worthwhile to sell— but you crossed that hurdle a few pages back.

Many business owners are very poor at self-promotion. Some are quite shy. Others were brought up to be very modest. We are supposed to keep our light 'under a bushel' in some parts of our society. We are afraid that people may say we are 'pushy'. We often learn bad habits in the jobs we had before we owned a business. Work miraculously appeared in the in-tray or on the factory line or in the workshop. But it doesn't just happen.

Now you have to find the work as well as do it. Sales is in your position description now, even if it never was before. And even if you have good people selling in your business, you should never leave it to them.

As the business owner, you carry weight and status that no employee can. This is especially true when it comes to networking. Other business owners will want to meet you, both formally and informally. Knowing and dealing with the owner is attractive to others.

The types of networks that work will vary with your business. If you operate in a small town, you should almost certainly join one of the local service clubs, such as Rotary. Other business owners and senior managers will also belong and these are the people who can make the decision to bring their business's business to you.

You should almost certainly network in a more formal business way (for example, through a Chamber of Commerce) with other owners of small businesses—to discuss what is going on in your area, to support each other, to keep each other in the loop about planning activities and so on that might affect your businesses. You can even be a very effective lobby group on occasion. All these ties will lead to more business for you—assuming that you are deserving of the business in the first place.

Owners of small businesses can become very isolated; you are busy and it is easy to put your head down and ignore the bigger arena for your sales. If you want to grow your business, you will need to be well connected. Friends, associates, connections—all play an important role in getting you contracts and invitations to tender for business. When community groups consider new ventures, they will want the business to go to a good local citizen.

The challenges of growth

Growth is not free. Your business may have to wear additional costs or invest heavily in order to grow. This is not without risk—the growth strategy might take a long time to fire or could even fail. If you have borrowed to fund your growth, you may be quite exposed for a while. None of these risks should put you off; they should instead make you do your planning carefully and take a managed approach to growth.

Not all growth is good. Growth that causes cost blowouts in terms of overtime, penalties that arise from not meeting your deadlines, and customer dissatisfaction with your erratic performance is not good for your business. Your reputation is at stake. Nobody cares about how hard it is for you—they only see the end results.

Cash flow is another key area to keep an eye on. When you are in a growth phase, you may need a great deal more working capital to fund day-to-day operations. You may have to increase stock levels or take on additional staff. You will almost certainly have more customers or clients and perhaps have provided far more credit. It pays to anticipate all of this and to plan well. You may need to increase your overdraft facilities and you should do this in good time. Banks are notoriously fair-weather friends—you do not want to be asking them for additional help when you are already in trouble. The strains on cash flow that often follow a period of growth have put an end to many a business. Don't let it happen to you.

Beware, too, of the Casanova syndrome—wooing and lavishing attention on the new customer and neglecting the old, once-loved client. It is very common to see businesses put all of their efforts into new business and become very complacent about the loyal customers that have made them successful. Clients are often treated as 'captive'—the business considers that it has their custom forever. This is almost never true. I get asked over and over again to recommend new accountants, lawyers, risk advisors, investment specialists and bankers. No doubt, the ones who have the business complacently believe that they have my client in the bag and have stopped making any effort for them. They are too busy chasing after new loves. Little do they know that divorce is planned! The ignored and spurned will never forgive you and their vengeance will be terrible. It is extremely wasteful to lose existing clients. Apart from any other consideration, it is far, far more expensive to find new business than to keep existing business. Watch that your remuneration, commission or incentive systems are not unwittingly encouraging this behaviour by rewarding 'new' business but doing nothing to recognise and retain existing business.

Measure your rate of growth

Keep an eye on your rate of growth. The easiest way to measure it is to compare sales from one year (or preferred period) to the next.

On the one hand, you need to be aiming for some growth in order to make more money and take you closer to your goals of wealth and freedom. On the other hand, you don't want a rate of growth that is so rapid that it will damage your business, perhaps irretrievably. This is a particular vulnerability for a young business: the business owner cannot believe the good fortune of all the new sales, but often these are well beyond the capacity of the business to manage—you can't make or fund these sales, your quality may suffer, or you take your eye off some other critical indicator like debtors and all of a sudden a write-off puts you in real trouble. The bank will be unsympathetic—they have seen it too often and they have no interest in funding failure, only in recovering their money with as little loss as possible.

Growth in itself is not enough: you need *profitable* growth. So don't stop at measuring your top line. Keep an eye on your gross margins and make sure that you are not attaining growth by discounting your prices or becoming sloppy with your management of costs. Your gross profits have to pay for everything else in the business; if you let these slip, you will have no increase in net profits at all—and maybe even a *loss*!

You will also need to watch your net profit. The additional staff, confusion and general turmoil that tends to surround rapid growth often means that the business owner stops watching internal costs and expenses closely. You may find that you have far more revenues, but that the business is gobbling them up even faster. Sales expenses and other staffing are special targets to watch. And if growth is taking you out of the business for much of the time, you need to keep a very vigilant eye on administration. Remember, too, that when your business is growing rapidly there is often a lot of cash sloshing around. This can provide a great deal of temptation if your controls are not very tight. The younger your business, the less likely that good controls or experienced people are in place to prevent slippage in these areas. This infrastructure (what we called 'bureaucracy' in our old jobs!) is essential to keep the business safe. The more externally focused and entrepreneurial the owner, the more likely they are to fail to see these problems until late in the story. I don't wish to sound cynical here, only to pass on some hard-won experience. You wouldn't be the first (and you won't be the last) to find yourself exuberant with the successful growth of your business, only to have it all come crashing down because of easily avoidable problems like these.

You may not believe you are a great numbers person—and you don't have to be a mathematical whiz. This is only primary school arithmetic. A few numbers will tell you everything you need to know. You can spot trends quickly if you monitor these numbers and you can take action to change course or stop the rot. You won't need to look at many other numbers if the key ones are right. There is an added benefit: if people see you monitor these numbers regularly, they will monitor their own behaviour much more carefully, saving you lots of time and trouble.

6

Cashing in

Looking to the future

Sometime in the future, you will no longer be running or owning the business. You may reach a point where you want to work fewer hours and have others involved in management responsibilities. You may want involvement and responsibility, but less hands-on and day-to-day management. You may also want to get some or all of your money out of the business. There may be several reasons for this. You may want to release money for lifestyle, such as a new home or travel. You may realise that too much of your wealth is still tied up in the business and that that is not a risk you can afford to take as the years go on.

Deciding what you want for the future is the first step.

Right now, you may see owning and running the business as one and the same thing, but of course they are different, with different responsibilities. They can also be easily separated, even if you have always combined the two until now.

Who will buy your business?

It is worth considering prospective buyers from the outset. Typically, buyers come from the following groups—family, competitors, suppliers, customers, employees, or others with lump sums, such as retirees or people who have received big redundancy payouts. Some businesses may be sold to corporates or can even be floated publicly. The end buyers should be considered from the start. What will they look for? What will they want to buy? What might put them off? What does this mean for your business—how do you build and groom your business so that it is attractive to the groups that are most likely to purchase it?

Competitors typically purchase other businesses in their industry to grow their market share. Your business may have built up a good customer base that your competitor would like, or you may have developed brands or a position in the market that would fit very well with the competitor. Competitors are usually in a very good position to evaluate how good your business is, as they are seeing the consequences of your success each day. They may be interested in purchasing your business simply to keep another player out. The volume of your business may give them the critical mass they need to grow their own business further.

Suppliers and customers are similar, as they are both involved in the chain of industry that surrounds your business. Suppliers or customers are often interested in a business because they want to operate in a bigger part of the value chain of the industry. They probably feel that they understand the business and industry well enough to play in other parts of it—which is not always the case. They are usually close enough to your business to evaluate how well you do what you do, and they usually have a good base of comparison as they supply or purchase from your competitors as well. They are in a good position to see what you consume and envisage themselves supplying their own needs or see the healthy profits you are making from selling to them and want a share of that action.

Employees, especially key ones, are in a very good position to understand the business and how it is run. Often key employees have been in the business for several years. They know how to make and deliver the product or service, they have good relationships with the customers and they know that they could continue to run the business at a healthy profit. After all, they may have been managing the business in your absence for years. No doubt, employees also have ideas about what they could change to increase profits or grow the business. Employees often lack the finance to purchase the business. If you have a good manager or a suitable team of employees, you might want to consider grooming them for running the business. Money may be a problem, but with your support they ought to be able to deal with the bank. You might want to consider leaving some money in the business for a while or having a staged sell-down.

Retirees and those with redundancy payments often seek to buy a business because they want to create an income and they may not be ready or able to live off their lump sums. Farming couples that have sold the farm often seek a business in a nearby town or in a holiday spot where they already own a home. These people may never have run a business in your industry before—or indeed, have never run any kind of business other than the farm. They will be seeking something that looks simple to run, that provides good cash and that will use their time and skills well. Generally, they will be seeking a small, simple business, as they usually have neither the cash nor the expertise to run a more complicated one.

Corporates frequently swallow up smaller businesses, either because you have developed a foothold in an area of business that they would like to enter or because you have some particular expertise or technology that they want to acquire. For example, big breweries swallowed some microbrewers because they saw a new trend in the marketplace that they needed to be involved in. Buying an existing business allows them to leapfrog years of planning, development and investment and get right in now. Likewise, your business may be hurting a corporate— nibbling away at one of their products or services or dominating a locality. The easiest thing to do is to take you out—and they may even acquire some valuable processes and customers as a result. Corporates usually buy because it is easier and cheaper than fighting you over the years it would take. Corporates are usually uninterested in very small businesses— you have to take your business to a certain level before it is likely to attract their interest.

Family members may well be interested in taking over the business. After all, they may have grown up with it and may already be deeply involved. Many entrepreneurs really want the business to stay in the family and be passed on to sons and daughters and even to the next generation. These can be very emotional issues for families and add a level of complication to all of the usual business and financial decisions. You may well have grown the business with this future in mind and have been training and grooming some of your children for this role for years. If this is the path you are on, it is very important to have family conversations about these intentions as early as possible. I have seen some very upset business owners (and entire families) when the founder finally discovered that the children wanted no part of the business and did not want to take on the responsibility of ownership.

Family succession needs to start early—years before the owner intends to hand over the full reins of management and partial or full ownership. You need to talk openly and honestly about what each individual wants for the future and how each of you sees this working. Younger people are often very frustrated at being treated like children and may leave in order to achieve and succeed elsewhere in a time frame that suits them. If one or more of your children is to succeed you, they will need lots of varied experience in the business to build competence and confidence. In addition, other staff will need to see that they really deserve the roles they are being given. Depending on your business, they may need external training and development, such as formal education, business courses and perhaps even roles in other businesses. All of this takes time and planning and cannot be left until the last minute.

Business owners often find the concept of 'selling' the business to family a difficult one. They often feel that they should be able to hand it on as an inheritance. You may well want to do this—after all, it is your business and your money! However, many business owners cannot afford to hand over the business unencumbered; it is usually their sole source of income and may hold almost all of their wealth. With help from an accountant, you and your children should be able to agree on a value for the business and make arrangements for buying you out. This can happen over several years and can be on whatever terms you agree. However, it is very important that your wealth and income are safeguarded for the future. Remember, you went into business and took all those risks so that you could finish wealthy and free!

Whom of the above is most likely to buy your business? Have the likely buyers shown any interest? Have you signalled that you might be willing to sell one day? Have you thought about how your business looks from their point of view?

Creating a saleable business

You don't have to sell your business—after all, it's yours to do with what you want. However, I think you should aim to create a business that is *saleable*. A saleable business is more valuable than one that no one wants to buy. If you own a business that is not saleable, you are dependent on working for wages and whatever profits you can manage from the business. You can never stop under this scenario unless your profits are so high for several years that you create enough wealth outside of the business through other investments to set you free.

A saleable business will be providing wages and probably profits too. But in addition, it will be worth something—hopefully enough to allow you to start living the life of your dreams. Creating a saleable business gives the business owner an eventual way out.

Businesses can be developed or run in ways that make them more saleable. A potential buyer will be considering critical factors, such as how dependent the business is on the founder, the talent and skill of staff, the quality of the systems and processes in place, and the difficulties of running the business. If the business owner is thinking clearly about an ultimate sale, these factors (and more) can be shaped in a way to facilitate rather than hinder sale. You make lots of choices as you shape and grow your business. You can choose to make your business more rather than less saleable—and it makes sense to make it more attractive to potential buyers. After all, the more saleable your business is, the more choices you have for the future.

The key to selling anything is to make it easy to buy. Let's consider some of the factors that may affect saleability.

Dependence on the founder

If the business is built entirely around you, it will be difficult to sell. This seems obvious, as no one else can become you, so buyers will wonder if there is any real 'business' without you. Business owners often make the business entirely dependent on them without realising that is what is happening. Consider, for example, a business that is built around your particular skills and experience. No one else may have the same mix or even understand what it is that you do. Sometimes the business owner holds all of the key relationships with customers or clients. Their loyalty may be to that particular person rather than to the business, and a buyer knows that all of this custom may be at risk once the original owner sells. If much of the goodwill of the business is attached to the owner, it will also lower the potential sale price.

Many business owners run their business around themselves. They are there every day and are involved in almost everything or have to be available to make many of the decisions. A good test is to ask how often and for how long you can be away from your business on holidays. If you find it difficult to leave the business for any length of time, it may be that you have made the business overly dependent on you. You should take steps to change that, perhaps involving other people or creating systems that allow you to be absent. No one will want to buy a business if they see that they will be tied to it every week for ever.

Staff

The business does not own its staff and of course they may choose to leave at any time. However, a prospective buyer will look at the other people in the business. They will want to see competent staff who do a good job, are liked by clients and customers and who have lots of knowledge about the business. Many buyers may not want to work full-time (or even at all) in the business and so will want to see that staff can be left unsupervised to get on with the job. They will be hoping to find at least one other person who understands the business as well as you do and is capable of doing most of the management tasks. A potential buyer will be put off by poor-quality staff and wonder why you have allowed such people to work in your business. They will certainly not want to take on badly trained or unhappy staff, as they will understand that this will make the business very difficult for them to run profitably.

Systems and processes

Because many business owners have set up everything themselves, the business systems often remain in their heads. This poses great barriers for a buyer, as they do not know the detail of how your business works. Sometimes the founder likes being the repository of all information, as that can boost the ego or make the founder feel that they are in control. However, keeping everything in your head is very dangerous for the business because it puts the business at risk if anything, such as illness, happens to you. It also makes the business inefficient, as everyone has to keep running to the owner for information and decisions that they should be able to make on their own. Potential buyers want to see a business that is under control and that will run well without the minute-by-minute intervention of the owner. Key systems and processes, such as how you manufacture things, how you sell, how you manage debtors and how you manage your customer database, should all be documented and set up to work with or without you. It will impress a potential buyer if your business seems to run itself, with important things happening on monthly, weekly and daily cycles and with documentation (on screen or paper) that staff can refer to as necessary. Think of it as having your business 'in a box'—it will really impress.

Without good systems and processes, a potential owner knows they are buying a headache. After all, it would probably be easier to set up from scratch than to take over your business and then spend months trying to figure out how it all fits together.

Records

Potential buyers will want to see good records. What they expect will vary with the business, but at the very least you should have your Certificate of Incorporation, your accounts and tax filings for several years and any pieces of paper that are critical to the business, such as contracts with suppliers or customers, joint venture agreements, partnership agreements, employment contracts, position descriptions, health and safety records and minutes of important meetings. It is expensive, and often very difficult, to replace some of the above. In addition, not keeping good records makes you look poorly organised and a potential buyer will suspect that the business is also poorly organised. A buyer wants a clean business; shoddy record-keeping will raise suspicions that you have done other important things shoddily as well.

Size

Size can seem like a strange factor for saleability. However, most buyers will expect to make a living from the business, so it will need to be big enough to provide at least a very good wage and hopefully some profits. Equally, buyers will not want a business that is too big for them to run alone but not big enough (not high enough revenues or margin) to justify employing staff. So, if you have set up your business to give you a low wage and it needs you to work 70 hours a week to keep it going, only a fool will take it over. You may have done it out of love, but a buyer will use different criteria! Size will also matter in terms of how it affects value. Many groups, such as employees or cash buyers who have sold a farm or been made redundant, will be looking for a smaller business (valued between $1 million and $3 million), while corporates or large suppliers/customers will be looking for something large enough to give them a firm toehold in the market. If you have potential buyer groups in mind, consider how big you should grow the business and try to avoid ending up caught between two stools.

Name and appearance

The look of your business and the name over the door are unlikely to be make-or-break issues, but it makes sense to appeal to the prospective buyers rather than turn them off. Many entrepreneurs call the business after themselves—Jim Smith Engineering or Jane Bloggs Design. It seems to make sense at the time and it is flattering to the ego. However, it makes it all the harder for the business to survive you—even your son or daughter is likely to have a different name. We can all point to international brand names that originated with a family name, such as Ford, Myer and Heinz, but even they restricted themselves to a surname. So it pays to be careful about what you put over the door. The look of your business can matter too. The more your business deals directly with customers on the premises, the more appearance counts. It is obvious that the beauty salon or car showroom should look attractive, neat and clean. But there is no reason for a factory or engineering workshop to look a mess either. Prospective buyers will intuit much about your business from the premises, the signage, the appearance of staff and the order—or lack of it—they see when they visit.

Barriers to entry

Prospective buyers are attracted to businesses that have good barriers to entry; that is, businesses that are hard to copy or set up in competition against. Many things can provide a barrier to entry. The business may have secured the best location possible, for example. Other barriers are things like licences to manufacture or distribute a certain brand. Concessions are yet another barrier that is becoming increasingly important in the tourism industry—limited numbers of operators may be allowed in certain areas, for example. Proprietary processes or recipes may also be a barrier; for example, your business may have built a brand around food products and the recipe forms an effective barrier to competition. Barriers offer a great deal of protection and reassurance for the buyer and so make your business more saleable and more valuable. It is in your interest to develop as many barriers to entry as possible.

All of the above issues affect saleability. Look at your business through the eyes of a buyer. Identify possible issues that you may have and address them. They will improve your business anyway.

What is your business worth?

Many business owners have no idea what their business is worth. Some entrepreneurs dream of a big organisation arriving out of the blue some day and offering them millions for their invention or copyrights or total business. It's a nice dream, but it rarely happens.

Your business will be worth somewhere between very little and an awful lot. From a pragmatic viewpoint, it is worth what someone will pay for it—just like your house. There is a much bigger market for houses than businesses, however, as almost everyone needs a home but comparatively few people need a business. It is easier to value houses, as more of them sell every week and you can compare yours to a similar one in a similar area.

Understanding how buyers and bankers value businesses is useful. It lets you evaluate the worth of your business and it encourages you to think about ways you could make the business more valuable.

When someone buys a business, they are really buying a stream of earnings. So, naturally the thing they will focus on is how much the business is earning at the moment. Buyers usually look at the profit a business is making before charges such as interest, tax and depreciation are applied. They are looking to see what kind of earnings the business can produce. Usually, the business is valued at some multiple of those earnings. Small businesses are usually bought at three to five times earnings. Shares on the share market are valued like this too: the earnings of the company are divided by the number of shares to give an earnings per share number. Buyers buy shares by deciding how many times earnings they are willing to pay. Some shares have a very high price to earnings ratio (P:E) because buyers think they are worth fifteen or twenty times earnings, while others have a lower P:E of five to ten times earnings because purchasers don't believe that the future earnings are as reliable or as high.

Several factors can affect the multiple that you are paid for your business earnings. If your business has a good record of good earnings for several years, it will be more valuable than one that is just getting on its feet. So your profits for the preceding years matter. Some owners try to keep profits down in order to minimise tax: this can backfire on you when you come to sell. Buyers want to buy a profitable business with a good track record.

The state of your industry can affect the value of the business. When technology stocks were still very fashionable, higher multiples were paid for businesses in that sector—the dotcom boom that became a crash. At the time of writing, petrol prices are escalating sharply. This will presumably affect the value of businesses that use a lot of fuel or that might be seen to boom at times like this, such as refining.

Buyers like to see a rising sales graph. They are, of course, hoping to continue to grow the business and are unlikely to be attracted to a business that seems to have plateaued. On the other hand, they may look at a slow business and see lots of opportunities to cut costs, grow sales and expand the business. They may be happy to buy this business, but you wouldn't expect to get a high multiple of earnings.

When the business is valued on its earnings like this, the owner gets paid for running the business well over the years.

Sometimes a business is valued on its net assets. This approach involves working out what the business would be worth if you closed it down and sold what it owns— buildings, vehicles, equipment and so on. Some businesses have lots of valuable assets, while others have few. Sometimes the assets are worth more than the earnings, particularly if they can be sold off separately. That's what corporate raiders do—find a business that's worth more than its share price and then break it up and strip out all of the assets. Sometimes they make a killing, but all they have done is recognise what others did not—that the business was worth more in pieces than it was all together. This can happen because a business is badly run, or because times have changed and the market has overtaken the business. It may have been a great business in the past. A business with lots of buildings or land in a good location or with a fleet of vehicles may well be valued on its assets rather than on earnings.

Goodwill is the other component that adds value to your business. Buyers buy earnings and assets. These are tangible and real. Goodwill is a term for all of the other things that might have value in a business, such as reputation, brand names, licences you hold and relationships that the business has. Sometimes buyers will pay a lot for goodwill in a business. It's a premium that can make you wealthy and free.

Creating goodwill

Goodwill is a premium that you may get for running your business well. It is not unusual for buyers to pay a great deal more than the business valuation, which was based on earnings or on assets. As we have discussed in the previous chapter, prospective buyers of a business are looking to buy profits. They are also often buying tangible assets such as plant, stock and vehicles.

But *intangible* assets have a value too. These are non-physical assets such as reputation, brands, history, licences, systems or concessions. Sometimes these may be very valuable indeed. For example, think of the value of the Coca-Cola brand or the recipe for KFC chicken. A business that is open, has good customers and has a track record of operations does have value. The buyer does not have to go through all the hassles of a start-up. It is clear that there is a market and that the location works. Staff are employed and there will be revenues and profits from day one. In short, it is a going concern and buyers will pay a premium for that valuable, but fairly intangible, asset.

Accountants see goodwill as the difference between the price paid for the business and the valuation of the assets. From your point of view, getting as much extra for goodwill as you can is highly desirable. Goodwill may provide the additional money that will make you wealthy and set you free.

Some industries attract little goodwill; for example, many forms of consultancy. The loyalty tends to attach to the consultant and without him or her there is little to sell. Many of these types of businesses are really forms of self-employment, as there are neither tangible assets to sell nor any goodwill attached to the business. Consultants can, of course, make a lot of money from their 'business', but it is in the form of ongoing income rather than in the creation of a capital asset that they can sell. You can't sell a career!

You should attempt to create as much goodwill in your business as possible. Consider the following elements.

Reputation

What is the reputation that your business has in your area of influence? Are you seen as first choice? Good value? Reliable? Good to do business with? Find out what your reputation is and do what you need to do to make it what it should be. A great proportion of business is done on word-of-mouth advertising. Think about how you and your friends talk about places to eat or visit. Be sure that you know what people are saying about your business and that it is what you want them to say. You will get a good return on this when you sell.

Brands

Brands are an aspect of reputation. Your business name may be the brand or your business may have several brands. You might, for example, be in the automotive trade and have a brand for your saleyard, a brand for maintenance and repairs, a brand for customising vehicles and a brand for parts. One of these brands may be far superior to the others—the rest being supporting acts. While your business may do several things, and may have to cover costs and keep the work flowing in, you need to decide what you are really good at and build that brand.

Being known for something special is part of building up the value that is goodwill.

Agencies, licences and concessions

Many businesses will have an agency to distribute other products or a licence to use certain technology or a concession to represent another major brand. These have value. If appropriate, you should seek to obtain these for your business and to have exclusive rights in your area. Possession of these will make your business more valuable when you want to sell down.

Processes, recipes, in-house technologies and systems

Intangible assets that you can develop in your business can create value in the form of goodwill. Depending on your business, these might be recipes for things you make, processes for delivering services, systems for running the business better or even proprietary technologies that your business invents.

Making your business more valuable for sale

Checklist

- **Maximise your profit margin** Business owners often try to hide profits! Recast your profits to show what you are taking out of the business, so that a potential buyer can see what a good business it really is. Eliminate non-essential spending as you approach the years of sale—given that the price will most likely be a multiple of net profit, it does not make sense to have profits any lower than they might be. This is particularly true of expenditure that is designed to lower tax.

- **Maximise sales**   Prospective buyers love to see a rising sales graph. It is good if you can show a trend of growing sales that a buyer can imagine continuing.

- **Cut overheads**   Make your business look lean and well run. A buyer does not want to take on a mess or have to deal with overstaffing.

- **Tidy up your records**   Have the kind of records that a prospective buyer will want to see, including:
    - articles of incorporation;
    - share certificates and transfer journals;
    - documented minutes of regular board meetings;
    - tax filings;
    - position descriptions;
    - contracts of employment;
    - collective agreements;
    - confidentiality agreements;
    - service level agreements.

- **Size**   What's the right size for your business? Decide how big your business should be. Plan to grow the business or prune it to an attractive size and shape for sale.

- **Systems**   Are you creating systems that would allow another person to run your business? Make sure that the business does not reside in your head and that it is not solely reliant on you. Show buyers that they won't have to spend seven days a week in the business! The systems you need may be:
    - management systems (for example, to supervise your staff);

- sales systems (for example, to show approaches, rules and procedures);
- debtor management systems (for example, to collect money on time);
- planning systems (for example, for the operations and services you do);
- staffing (for example, who does what and how they relate);
- training (for example, what needs to be learned and how it is achieved);
- product and business development (for example, how you plan for improvement).

- **Appeal and appearance**   Has your business got appeal? Does the appearance of the buildings, vehicles and signage need treatment to make your business look its best?
- **Start well in advance of projected sale date**   It is always very difficult to know when is the right time to sell a business. You never quite know what the economy will do or what unforeseen events might occur in your industry, among your competitors or in your local area. A prospective buyer might appear any day, so you should think about all of these things well in advance of any sell date you might have in mind.
- **Groom the key indicators in years leading up to sale**   As an owner, you will have a feeling for the aspects of your business that buyers might find either attractive or off-putting. The principal way that a buyer will judge your business is through the numbers, so give yourself time to get these indicators in good shape to impress any prospective buyers.
- **Establish barriers to entry**   Make it as difficult as possible for a potential competitor to enter your patch. In that way,

you are more likely to keep them out, more likely to keep your profits up and more likely to have a buyer pay you a big premium to buy you out. Things that may provide barriers to entry include:

- *Location* Have you got a good location for your business? Look at how carefully businesses such as McDonald's and Starbucks choose their sites.
- *Proprietary products* Have you a product or service that you can offer that no one else has or that is better than anyone else's?
- *Intellectual property* Is there stuff that you know or can do that other competing businesses cannot or that would cost them a lot to copy?
- *Brand and reputation* Have you the reputation (or brand) that makes you difficult to take on? This might be a recognised (national) brand name or simply the accumulation of good history in your area.
- *Licences* Do you have a licence to produce or distribute a product or service good enough to ward off competition? This is often in the form of a franchise.

• **Can you make *your* business so good in *your* market that no one will take you on from scratch?** That's a killer question! If you can, someone is likely to pay you a lot of money to take you over or buy you out of the way.

Selling the business

Sooner or later, you are likely to want to sell down a share or sell out entirely. Hopefully, you have reached a stage where you have created enough wealth and now want to be free!

Business owners sell for many additional reasons and several of the following may also apply to you:

- **So that you can stop working so hard** You may or may not be ready to stop doing full-time paid work, but many business owners find it very hard to get away from the business for any decent length of time. You may want less responsibility, if any at all. You may want to work only a limited number of hours. Selling out or selling down may be your best option to get a different balance in your life.
- **For health reasons** Business owners are not generally wonderful at taking care of themselves. The same drive and the same huge spirit and energy that got you involved in a business may mean that you have continued to overdo it all your life. Getting out or passing on some of the responsibility may have become necessary to your wellbeing and enjoyment of life.
- **You have achieved what you wanted** Businesses often reach a stage or size where you know that you have done your bit and that it will take a different person with different skills to go on to the next stage. The entrepreneurs who start businesses often know in their hearts that they are the wrong person to take the business into the next phase—and they often don't want to. Consolidation and systematisation are often lacking in excitement for the entrepreneur.
- **It's time to do other things** Many business owners have deferred or put on hold other important aspects of their life and dreams. There comes a time when you know that you need to devote more energy to your partner, children, travel, contribution to society, hobbies and so on.

- **The death of a business partner**   Remaining partners often want to sell because they can't replace the expertise easily or may have to sell in order to pay the deceased's estate.
- **Other disasters**   Divorce may prompt a business sale in order to buy out a former spouse or partner.
- **Changes in the rules**   New legislation can often precipitate a business sale. New laws or local bylaws and regulations may make your business a target or may mean you can no longer compete as you are.
- **You have had enough**   You may have become bored, tired or just fed up with the relentless round of ownership and management. You could even be burnt out—it creeps up on so many. If the excitement is gone, it is usually time for a change.
- **Someone wants to buy you out**   These offers can come out of the blue. Sometimes changes in your industry or a competitor's expansion plans mean that others will offer to buy you out to get a foothold in the market or to increase their share or influence in your area. Offers may also come from members of your family, your business partner or some of your staff.

It is important to think about why you might sell and to think about it as early as you can, so that you can exit on your own terms and feel as much in charge of the process as possible. We have already discussed that it is important to think about possible sale early, in order to have the business in good shape and maximise the sale price. But early preparation is important from a personal point of view also, so that you and other affected people are as prepared as possible. Family can obviously be affected, as selling down or out may represent a huge change in your family life. Should a business partner or family member be taking on more ownership or management responsibility, they too will need time to prepare.

One of the other disconcerting aspects of a sale is that it may come out of the blue. You may have targeted a date years hence, but are approached by a buyer in the meantime. This can throw many business owners into a state of turmoil. It pays to be ready for a sale at any time. Have your paperwork up to date and be ready to present your business well to a buyer. It would be silly to miss or pass by the opportunity to sell at a good price just because you never expected it and could not come to terms with the idea quickly. Emotional readiness is as important as having the business in a presentable state for potential buyers.

It is always difficult to time the sale perfectly. Ideally, you will want to do this when the economy and the conditions in your industry are favourable. These factors are beyond your control, but you need to have your business in the best condition for sale long before you anticipate wanting to get out. You never know the day you will want to sell down or out because of unanticipated changes in your life. On the other hand, you never know when a prospective buyer will make you an offer out of the blue. But whenever you want to sell or someone else wants to buy, it is in your interest to have the business in the best shape so as to maximise sale value. Well-run businesses are *always* more valuable.

There are several issues you may want to consider when you are approaching a sale:

- **Using a broker or intermediary** Business brokers operate like real estate agents and usually have several businesses and several prospective buyers on their books at any time. Brokers are usually retained and paid by the seller. The broker can advertise on your behalf or keep the sale confidential by dealing only with interested buyers (rather than publicising your plans to clients, customers, staff and others to the detriment of your business in the meantime). The broker can screen genuine buyers from the rest and protect you from 'fishing expeditions' by competitors. Brokers can also draft the contract of sale, but you should make sure your lawyer gives it approval. Brokers are usually paid on commission and you need to be aware of that, as it can mean that your best interests are not necessarily uppermost. Anyone can set up as a business broker, so you need to choose carefully.

- **What exactly you are selling—Shares? Assets? Going concern?**
- **Contract of sale**
- **Valuation** The business can be valued in a number of ways, including assessing the assets or applying a multiple to earnings, or a combination. You may want to get an independent valuation in order to confirm your estimate.
- **Financing the sale**
- **Confidentiality agreements**
- **Non-compete agreements**

It can be very difficult to sell your business when you have spent years establishing and nurturing it. Emotion can easily cloud your judgement at this time. Many owners think the business is worth more than it is, for example. This is a very good time to be surrounded by trusted advisers. Take their advice.

Planning for life *after* the sale

Owners can spend so much of their life building and nurturing their business that it becomes very hard for them to envisage a life without the business. This can make it very hard to let go and often results in poor preparation for selling or exiting the business. Unfortunately it can also mean that owners miss good times or opportunities for the sale of the business, which can have disastrous consequences for their future financial security.

Just as it is important to dream and plan for the future of a business, it is essential that the business owner has dreams and plans for life beyond the business. Early on, start thinking about how you would like to live life once you have little or no involvement in the business. What will you choose to be doing? Where will you choose to live? How will you spend your time? What has been on hold or neglected for years that you will now choose to devote time and energy to?

Many owners choose to have an ongoing involvement in the business, if that is appropriate. They may mentor the new owner, who may be a family member or former employee. If you have significant money (by way of a loan or shares) still invested in your business, you may wish to retain a role as chair of the board. This would mean that you would attend regular meetings and maintain an overarching responsibility for financial performance and direction for the future.

Others may choose to contribute their considerable business experience elsewhere, perhaps as a director in another business, as a coach or mentor (paid or voluntary), or even in a teaching capacity at a local institute.

It can be a very good idea to plan a long holiday with family or friends to mark the transition from business owner to your new life. This has the benefit of placing a stake in the ground— you have made commitments to others for travel and so on that you must keep. It also allows the new regime to settle in to the business without you, as it can be a very difficult time for the new managers as they begin to establish themselves.

It is wise to plan how you will spend your time for the first several months. Business owners are usually vigorous people with lots of talents and energy. There are often many other things that they wish to do that they have put aside for years. Family, friends and members of your network will also have requests for your new-found time. You might, for example, commit to playing golf several times a week and prepare for this by renewing your club membership and buying new clubs. Others might enrol in a program of study or commit time to a not-for-profit organisation of their choice. Before long you are likely to wonder how you found the time to run a business! However, it is important to recognise that the transitional period is the most difficult—you are used to being busy, so it will help to have some structure initially.

Make your plans for life after the sell down of the business as compelling as possible. It is much easier to move *towards* activities and commitments that you want to participate in rather than move *from* the routines and responsibilities that have filled your life for many years in business. Never forget that the reason you owned a business was to create financial freedom—the wealth *and* time to live the life you choose. Now is that time.

Last word

We are surrounded by examples of successful businesses. Most of the rich and free have become so through a business rather than luck. Business opportunities take commitment and hard work and you need to be willing to take risks, but the rewards can be great.

If 'luck' exists, it is about being ready to take advantage of opportunity. And opportunities strike all the time. Being prepared for business opportunities involves understanding the kind of business model you need, how to work on your business and how to improve profits and foster growth. Will you be one of the people who take advantage of the opportunities presented by creating and running your own business?

Most importantly, you need to understand why you are in business in the first place. Understanding why you own a business will keep you focused on the endgame—creating a valuable business that will set you free and fund the lifestyle that you want. Nothing less is sufficient reward for the investment of time and talent and the risks you have taken.

It is up to you. You don't have to be in business. You can settle for ordinary. Or you can choose to become rich and free through your business. It will take effort and energy and there is always more to learn. You don't have to found a global corporation or establish a national brand; you only have to create a better than average business in your own area in order to do extremely well. And you have to be ready and willing to act.

So get ready. Decide to live the dream. Make yourself rich and free through owning your own business.